Encyclopedia of
Ocean
Life

Encyclopedia of
Ocean
Life

Sally Morgan

Sandy Creek
NEW YORK

Sandy Creek
NEW YORK

An Imprint of Sterling Publishing
387 Park Avenue South
New York, NY 10016

© 2008 by Parragon Books Ltd
This 2012 custom edition is published exclusively for Sandy Creek by Parragon.

ISBN 978-1-4351-4351-7

Manufactured 05/12
Lot # 10 9 8 7 6 5 4 3 2 1

Cover images: all Getty Images

Contents

Introduction 7

The world's oceans 9

Beaches and shores 35

Coastal life 61

Coral reefs 87

Open oceans 113

The deep ocean 139

Polar waters 165

Oceans in danger 191

Some useful words 216

Web sites 219

Index 220

Introduction

Vast oceans cover much of Earth's surface. They are home to millions of different animals—from the massive blue whale to tiny microscopic animals that float in the water.

This book takes you on a voyage of discovery through these enormous areas of water. You can learn about waves and tides. You will find out about animals that live along the coasts, on colorful coral reefs, and in the open ocean—as well as the mysterious animals of the deep.

Finally, you can discover why the world's oceans are under threat and find out what is being done to protect them.

The world's oceans

Earth is often called the blue planet because more than two-thirds of its surface is covered by water. Most of this water is found in the oceans. Oceans are huge areas of water that are many thousands of feet deep in places. The oceans are home to billions of animals and plants.

Southern Ocean

The Southern Ocean surrounds Antarctica. Most of this ocean is over 13,100 feet (4,000 m) deep. It is a dangerous ocean with strong winds and massive icebergs.

Five oceans

There are five oceans. The largest is the Pacific Ocean, which stretches between the Americas, Australia, and the eastern coast of Asia. The smallest is the Arctic Ocean, which surrounds the North Pole.

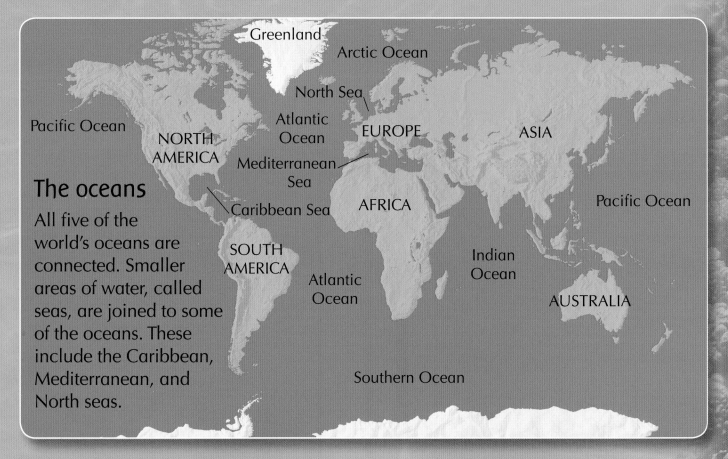

Greenland

Arctic Ocean

North Sea

Pacific Ocean

NORTH
AMERICA

Atlantic
Ocean

EUROPE

ASIA

Mediterranean
Sea

Pacific Ocean

Caribbean Sea

AFRICA

The oceans

All five of the world's oceans are connected. Smaller areas of water, called seas, are joined to some of the oceans. These include the Caribbean, Mediterranean, and North seas.

SOUTH
AMERICA

Atlantic
Ocean

Indian
Ocean

AUSTRALIA

Southern Ocean

Ocean islands

Oceans are mostly wide, empty areas of water. Islands are scattered across the open oceans. These pieces of land rise up from under the water. Islands may cover large areas of land or just a few square miles.

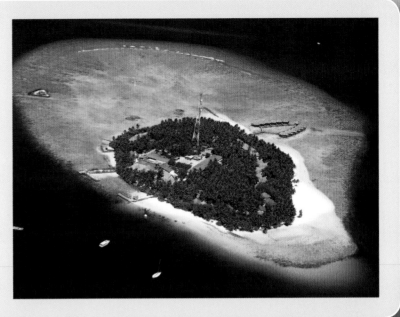

A small island in the Indian Ocean.

Coral reefs

Coral reefs are found off coasts and around islands in tropical parts of the world. Reefs are home to many kinds of fish and other colorful marine animals.

——— Coral reefs are built from the skeletons of tiny sea animals.

DID YOU KNOW?

The Pacific Ocean covers around 63.7 million square miles (165 million square km)—that's more than 15 times the size of the United States. The Arctic Ocean is just one and a half times the size of the USA.

Exploring the oceans

The first boats were built more than 40,000 years ago from wood and animal skin. As boats became larger, people traveled away from the safety of the coast to explore the oceans.

Ancient Egyptians

The ancient Egyptians built wooden boats that they sailed in the Mediterranean Sea. They may have sailed over 600 miles (1,000 km) along the coast of Africa to present-day Ethiopia.

Map making

The first maps of the world were drawn in the fifteenth century when much of the world was still unexplored. As explorers discovered new lands, the maps were updated.

DID YOU KNOW?

In 1760, clock maker John Harrison invented the chronometer. It was a special clock that could keep time at sea, and it enabled sailors to work out their east–west position.

This dhow is similar to the boats sailed by the ancient Egyptians.

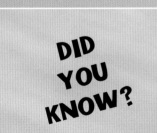

Sir Walter Raleigh

In 1584, English explorer Sir Walter Raleigh sailed across the Atlantic Ocean and set up the first English settlement in North America. Many years later he explored the coast of South America.

Astrolabe

This early navigational tool is called an astrolabe. Sailors used an astrolabe to work out how far north or south they were from the equator. To do this, they needed to align the sighting rule in the middle of the disk with the Sun.

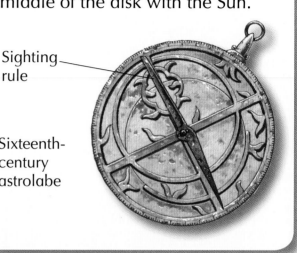

Sighting rule

Sixteenth-century astrolabe

Captain Cook

James Cook was captain of the first European ship to land in Australia. His ship *Endeavour* left England in 1768 and sailed across the Pacific and around New Zealand before discovering Australia. He came ashore at Botany Bay, Australia, in 1770.

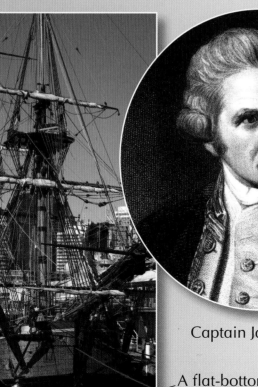

Captain James Cook

A flat-bottom hull allowed *Endeavour* to sail in shallow water.

Breakers

When waves reach shallow water near a coast, they slow down and become taller. Finally, the crest, or top, of the wave topples over and crashes down onto the shore.

Waves

Waves are created by wind blowing over the surface of the water. The stronger the wind, the bigger the waves. Waves travel across the ocean, just like ripples cross a pond.

Tsunamis

Tsunamis are waves made by earthquakes under the ocean. By the time the waves hit the coast, they may be many feet tall. Powerful tsunamis can cause a lot of damage.

Bow waves

Large waves form at the bow, or front, of a boat as it moves through water. During stormy weather, waves break over the bow and crash down on the deck.

Surfing

Riding a surfboard on the crest of a wave is an exciting sport. Skilled surfers can twist and turn, jump in the air, and ride their boards right under the wave as it rises up and curls over.

DID YOU KNOW?

In 1993, a tsunami struck the island of Hokkaido, Japan. The waves were about 98 feet (30 m) tall—as high as a 10-storey building.

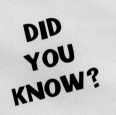

In 2004, a tsunami caused a lot of damage to this village in Banda Aceh, Indonesia.

Tides

Twice a day, the sea rises up a shore and then falls back again. High tide is when the sea reaches its highest point up a shore and low tide is when it is at its lowest point on the shore.

Low tide

At low tide, the sea exposes the whole of the shore. In some places, the difference between high and low tides is great, but in others it is very small.

The Sun and the Moon

The tides are caused by the pull of the Sun and the Moon. This pull is called gravity, and it pulls Earth's oceans toward the Sun and Moon. This creates a bulge of water that produces high tides. At the same time, there is less water in other parts of the ocean and this is what causes the low tides.

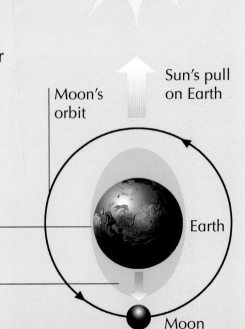

Sun

Moon's orbit

Sun's pull on Earth

Earth

Moon

Less water at low tides.

Bulge of water produces high tides.

Wading birds

Wading birds, such as oystercatchers and curlews (left), visit the coast at low tide to feed on small sea animals left uncovered by the tide. The birds poke in the mud or sand with their long bills, looking for worms and snails.

Resting place

The exposed areas of the shore are home to many creatures. Animals such as seals can use the seashore as a place to rest and breed.

Male elephant seals have a nose that looks a little like an elephant's trunk.

Ocean currents

Oceans are never still. Winds blowing over the surface of the oceans create flows of water called currents. These currents travel around the world.

Warm and cold currents

Currents of warm water flow from the equator toward the poles. Cold currents start in the Arctic and Antarctic and flow toward the equator.

Mild winters

Tropical palm trees can grow in this southern part of Great Britain (below) because there is a warm current flowing along the coast. This makes mild winters, and snow and frost are rare.

Arctic Ocean

Greenland

NORTH AMERICA

Atlantic Ocean

SOUTH AMERICA

Pacific Ocean

Southern Ocean

Warm current   Cold current

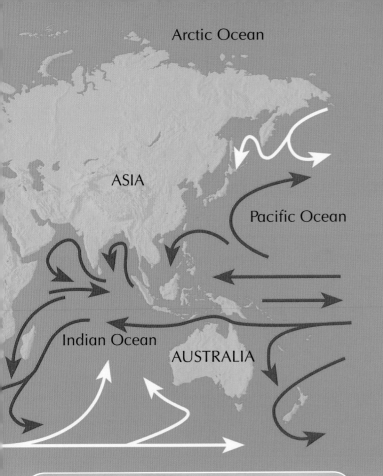

Arctic Ocean

ASIA

Pacific Ocean

Indian Ocean

AUSTRALIA

Plankton

Sometimes, an ocean current brings up a lot of food from the seabed. Tiny plants and animals called plankton feed well and increase in number, forming a plankton bloom. A plankton bloom can change the color of the water and measure several hundred miles across.

Plankton

DID YOU KNOW? The Gulf Stream is an ocean current that flows across the Atlantic Ocean from the Caribbean Sea to western Europe. It measures 50–90 miles (80–150 km) wide.

Plenty of fish

Some ocean currents are high in nutrients and encourage plankton to grow. This attracts fish that feed on the plankton. The large numbers of fish attract predators, such as seabirds.

A gull plucks a small fish from the water.

19

Ocean weather

Oceans play an important role in the world's weather. Tropical storms, hurricanes, and waterspouts all form over water.

Storm clouds gather over the Caribbean Sea.

Tropical storms

Rain falls most days in the regions nearest the equator, called the tropics. Storm clouds form off the coast during the day and bring a heavy downpour of rain at night.

The eye of the hurricane.

Hurricanes

Hurricanes are huge, spinning storms that form over warm water. Strong hurricane winds with speeds of up to 200 miles (320 km) per hour can cause a lot of damage if they move over land.

Monsoon

Each year, winds from the Indian Ocean bring heavy rain to Southeast Asia. These winds are called monsoons and they last several months. The monsoon season ends when the winds change direction and blow away from land.

Monsoon rains falling in India.

DID YOU KNOW?

On July 27, 2005, an amazing 37 inches (94 cm) of rain fell on Mumbai, India, in just 24 hours. This monsoon washed away thousands of homes, roads, and railroad tracks and killed more than 600 people.

Waterspout

A waterspout is a spinning column of air and water that moves over water. It looks just like a mini tornado. Although a waterspout is not as dangerous as a tornado, it can damage small boats.

Salt water

Seawater tastes very salty. This is because the water contains a lot of dissolved salt. Humans cannot drink seawater because it makes them ill. But animals that live in the sea have ways of coping with the high levels of salt.

Dried salt on the surface of a salt pan.

Salt pans

When salt water gathers in shallow ponds and the water dries up, it leaves behind large areas of salt called salt pans. The salt is collected and used for cooking.

Adding more salt

Some of the salt in seawater is from the breakdown of rocks and from hot-water vents on the ocean floor (see page 162). Volcanic eruptions under the oceans also add salt to the water.

Clouds of steam from an undersea volcanic eruption.

Albatross

The albatross can drink salt water because it has a special salt gland above its eye. The gland takes the extra salt from the bird's body and gets rid of it in a salty liquid that drips from its nostrils.

DID YOU KNOW?

The water in the Dead Sea in the Middle East is 10 times saltier than in the oceans. A person can float on the surface and not sink because the salty water is heavier than normal water and pushes harder against objects floating in it.

Turtle tears

Just like the albatross, turtles have a salt gland behind their eyes. By getting rid of salt through their eyes, nostrils, or tongue, turtles can live in salt water without becoming ill.

Living in water

Animals that live in water are called aquatic animals. Their bodies are adapted to life in water. Fish have gills to breathe under water, while seals have flippers to help them swim.

Sharks

Sharks are fish, and they breathe using gills. Water enters through their mouths and passes through the gills, where the oxygen is removed. Then the water leaves through the gill slits.

Most sharks have five gill slits on each side of their head.

Crabs

A crab has a heavy outer skeleton covering its body. A crab's body is quite flat so that it can easily squeeze between and under rocks.

Jellyfish

Jellyfish have soft bodies that are mostly made of water. They must stay in water to keep their shape. If you take them out of the ocean, they collapse into blobs like jello.

Seals

Seals are aquatic mammals with flippers instead of arms and legs. Although seals live in water, they breathe air and have to return to land to give birth.

Food chains

A food chain shows how nutrients pass from plants to animals as one eats the other. In the ocean, plant plankton are eaten by zooplankton, or animal plankton. The zooplankton are eaten by larger animals, and these animals are then eaten by even bigger animals.

Sharks

Many sharks have a diet of seals, turtles, fish, and even large seabirds. However, some sharks, such as the whale shark and basking shark, eat plankton and small fish.

Plant plankton

Plant plankton are at the bottom of the ocean food chains. They are called producers because they make their own food using sunlight.

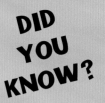

Plant eaters

Zooplankton, such as this crab larvae, are plant eaters. They eat the producers, or plant plankton. The plant eaters are known as primary consumers.

This great white shark has leapt out of the water to catch a seal.

Meat eaters

Larger animals called the secondary consumers eat the primary consumers. Secondary consumers are hunters. There are many different hunters in the ocean, including fish and squid.

Top meat eaters

Top carnivores, or meat eaters, such as pelicans (above), sharks, and dolphins, eat fish. A top carnivore is an animal that no other animal eats—they are at the top of the ocean food chain.

Beneath the surface

Imagine if you could walk into the sea from a beach. First you would walk through the shallow water of the continental shelf that extends out from the coast. Then the seabed slopes down for thousands of feet to the deep ocean floor.

Ocean levels

In some places, the continental shelf is narrow, but in other areas it stretches for hundreds of miles. The continental slope links the continental shelf with the ocean floor, which may be thousands of feet down.

Sea level

Continental shelf

Sea lions

Sea lions swim in the shallow water close to the shore above the continental shelf. They like to pull themselves out of the water and lie on sandy beaches.

Starfish

Starfish are found on the continental shelf. They crawl over the sand, hunting for mussels and other shellfish to eat.

28

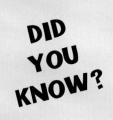
Hammerhead

Sharks, such as this hammerhead shark, are found in both shallow and deep water. Some sharks can dive down thousands of feet to the bottom of the oceans.

Different creatures are found at each depth of the ocean.

Spider crab

Spider crabs are creatures of the seabed. They have been found on the ocean floor over 10,000 feet (3,000 m) below the water's surface.

Continental slope

Ocean floor

Diving

People cannot live in water, but they can dive underwater. Divers can take a deep breath and swim underwater for a minute or so, but they need a supply of air to stay for longer.

Diving helmet

Early divers wore heavy diving helmets. Air was pumped from the surface into the helmets through rubber tubes.

Breathing underwater

Scuba divers carry a tank of air to breathe underwater. The tank is connected to a regulator, which the diver places in his or her mouth. When the diver breathes in, air flows through the regulator into the mouth.

Regulator

Exploring reefs

Many divers like to explore coral reefs. These are good places to find brightly colored fish and other marine creatures, such as dolphins and sea turtles.

Discovering wrecks

Shipwrecks in shallow water are popular dive sites. By exploring a wreck, divers can learn a lot about the history of the ship. They may even discover gold coins and other valuables in the wreckage.

This submersible has a strong frame made from titanium metal up to 2 inches (5 cm) thick.

Exploring the deep ocean

The deep ocean is very cold and the huge pressure would crush a human instantly. Scientists need hi-tech equipment to explore this part of the ocean.

Submersibles

Submersibles are specially designed mini submarines that can dive up to 15,000 feet (4,500 m) deep. Inside, there is room for only two or three people.

NORTH AMERICA

SOUTH AMERICA

ROVs

Remotely operated vehicles (ROVs) are controlled from the surface of the water. These vehicles have mechanical arms to pick up objects, and cameras to film any strange creatures.

Underwater features

Using technology such as submersibles, scientists have made maps of some of the ocean floor. They have found mountain ranges, such as the Mid-Atlantic Ridge, and deep valleys, such as the Mariana Trench in the Pacific Ocean.

EUROPE

Atlantic
Ocean

The Mid-Atlantic Ridge runs down the middle of the Atlantic Ocean.

AFRICA

Seastar

Comb jelly

Amphipod

DID YOU KNOW?

The Mid-Atlantic Ridge runs from Iceland to the Antarctic, and is more than 7,500 miles (12,000 km) long. It is the world's longest mountain range.

Deep-sea creatures

Scientists have discovered amazing creatures living deep underwater. They include seastars, blind shrimplike creatures called amphipods, and comb jellies, which can produce their own light.

Beaches and shores

The world's beaches and shores stretch for thousands of miles around every continent and island. There are rocky cliffs, sandy beaches, oozing mudflats, and hot mangrove swamps. The coast is a meeting place between the sea and the land.

Changing coasts

Coasts are never the same for very long. At high tide the shore is covered in salty seawater, while at low tide the coast is exposed to the sun and wind.

Rocky beaches

The constant battering of waves against a cliff wears away the rocks. Eventually, the cliff crumbles and rocks fall, creating a rocky beach. Over time, more and more rock ends up in the sea.

Groins

Protecting beaches

Groins are special walls built on a beach to protect the coast from battering waves. The groins slow down the waves and trap the shingle, or sand, so it is not carried away.

Sea arches

Soft rocks along a coast wear away faster than hard rocks, creating bays. The hard rocks form headlands. These headland rocks slowly wear away, first creating caves, then arches.

This sea arch has formed on the south coast of Great Britain.

Spits

A spit is a narrow strip of land that is formed when the tides remove sand from one beach and drop it farther along the coast.

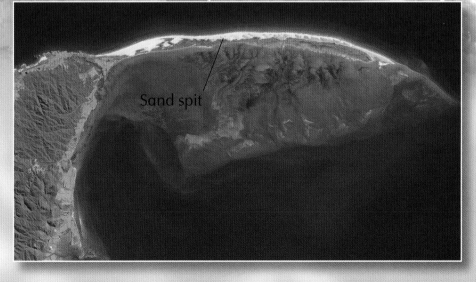

Sand spit

A sand spit in New Zealand

Rocky shores

When beaches are covered with rocks, they are called rocky shores. The rocks create a lot of hiding places for animals.

Tidal pools

When the tide goes out, water is trapped between the rocks. This creates tidal pools, cut off from the sea until the tide returns.

Rock shelters

Tidal pools are miniature worlds. They provide shelter for plenty of animals, such as starfish (left), snails, crabs, and barnacles. Some seaweeds also live in tidal pools.

Coastal creatures

Marine iguanas live in the cold Pacific Ocean around the Galápagos Islands. They are reptiles, which means that they are cold-blooded creatures. They come out of the water to sunbathe on the rocks and warm up.

Seaweed

Seaweeds cling to the rocks surrounding the pools. Small animals, such as crabs, snails, and fish, hide among the seaweed.

Blenny fish ———————————

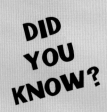

DID YOU KNOW?

The blenny, a small tidal-pool fish, is also called the sea frog because it likes to sunbathe on the rocks. It jumps back into the water with a plop if it is disturbed.

Surviving on the rocks

Life is tough on rocky shores when the tide goes out. The animals that live on the rocks have special ways to survive out of water.

Limpets have a dome-shaped shell that can survive the battering waves.

Limpets

Limpets feed on the tiny algae (plant life) that grows on the rocks. When the tide goes out, the limpets stick tight to the rocks so that they do not dry out.

Mussels

Mussels attach their shells to rocks. They have two shells that are hinged together. When covered by water, mussels open their shells and feed. When the tide goes out, they shut their shells tightly together for protection.

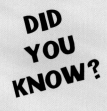

Tidal pooling

Tidal pools can be explored when the tide is out. However, you have to be careful not to get caught by the incoming tide and also not to slip on the rocks.

Sea anemones

Most sea anemones (below) do not like being uncovered by the tide. Some survive by pulling in their tentacles—they look like a blob of jello on the rock.

Tentacles

Cliff life

Cliffs tower above many shorelines. They are often windy places, sprayed with salty seawater. Life is difficult for the plants and animals that make their homes high on the rocks.

Towering cliffs

Cliffs are large lumps of rock that rise almost straight up from the shore. Most are less than 330 feet (100 m) tall, but in the Hawaiian Islands some cliffs are 3,300 feet (1,000 m) high.

Cliff plants

Cliff plants grow in gaps between the rocks. They grow close to the ground to stay out of the wind.

Living on a cliff

Cliffs are home to colonies, or groups, of seabirds such as gannets and kittiwakes. They like cliffs because predators, such as foxes and cats, cannot reach them. They lay their eggs on narrow ledges on the cliff's steep side.

These steep chalk cliffs are on the coast of Dover, Great Britain.

Seabirds nest on a cliff on the northern coast of Great Britain.

Puffins

Puffins live together in large colonies on cliff tops. They make their nests in long burrows that they dig in the soil.

43

Sandy shores

Tiny grains of sand are made as waves batter rocks into smaller and smaller pieces. Tides carry the sand along the coast and wash it up on the shore to form sandy beaches.

Traveling coconuts

Coconut palms are a common sight on tropical beaches. When coconuts drop into the sea, they are carried by the tide to other beaches, where they grow into new palms.

Sand colonies

Soft, sandy beaches are perfect places for many sea creatures, such as seals (above), to give birth. Seals raise their young in large colonies on the beaches.

Behind the beach

Winds from the sea blow sand inland. Small piles of sand soon build up around obstacles such as fences, plants, and stones. The piles of sand become gradually larger and, eventually, a sand dune is formed.

DID YOU KNOW?

Sand dunes are gradually blown inland by the wind. In some parts of France, sand dunes have buried whole villages.

Sea shells

Many sea animals have shells. When these animals die their soft body rots away, leaving behind the shell. Empty shells are often washed ashore. Shells of many different shapes and sizes can be found on beaches.

Living in sand

At first glance little seems to live on a sandy beach, but many different animals, such as crabs and snails, are hidden in the sand. They come out of hiding when the tide comes in.

Sand dollar

The sand dollar (above) is related to starfish and sea urchins. It has a flat body covered by spines, which it uses to burrow through the sand.

Weaver fish

Danger lurks in the sand. The weaver fish has poisonous spines, which stick up for protection when it has buried itself in the sand. Anybody who treads on it gets a very painful sting.

Tidal zones

The highest point reached by the tide is called the high-tide mark, and the lowest point is the low-tide mark. The shore between these two marks is divided up into the high-, mid-, and low-tide zones.

The spray zone lies above the high-tide zone.

High-tide mark

Spray zone

High-tide zone

Mid-tide zone

Low-tide zone

Low-tide mark

Coming out to feed

Animals such as the cockle hide from predators in the sand at low tide. They emerge when the tide comes in. Cockles are hunted by many animals, including crabs, birds, fish, and this colorful sun star (below).

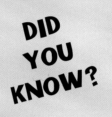

DID YOU KNOW? The razor shell gets its name from the shape of its shell, which is the shape of an old-fashioned cut-throat razor.

Cockle foot

The cockle can escape from predators by squirting a jet of water from its shell.

Scavengers

Waves wash seaweed and other marine debris up the beach, where it collects in a line at the high-tide mark. This is called the strand line.

Strand lines

The strand line is mostly a smelly mass of rotting seaweed, but it also contains dead bodies of fish and birds, and garbage from passing ships.

Scavenging crabs

Ghost crabs emerge from their sandy burrows in search of dead fish. They use their claws to tear the fish into small pieces that they can eat.

Strand lines along a beach in Thailand.

Sand fleas

Sand fleas (above) are among the smallest scavengers on the strand line. These flealike animals use their long legs to hop over the sand.

Coastal visitors

Sometimes, the dead bodies of whales and seals are washed up onto the shore. These attract animals such as brown bears and eagles. Bears that live by the coast often walk along the beach looking for food.

49

Nile Delta

Egypt

Nile River

Estuaries

Estuaries and deltas form where rivers flow into the ocean. Here, the fresh water of the river mixes with the salt water of the ocean.

The Nile Delta

The Nile Delta lies at the mouth of the Nile River in Egypt (left). Over thousands of years, the river has dropped large amounts of mud. This mud has built up into low-lying land, with a lot of channels of water leading out to sea.

River bends

As a river gets close to the sea, it gets wider and wider. It starts to weave about in large bends called meanders. The wide mouth of a river, where it meets the sea, is known as an estuary.

Sea otter

Some sea otters live in the shallow water of estuaries, where they hunt for crabs, mussels, and snails on the seabed. Sea otters often eat while floating on the surface of the water.

Webbed feet help sea otters swim easily through the water.

Feeding birds

The mud at a river mouth is full of worms and snails, which attract flocks of feeding birds. Birds use their long bills to find food in the mud.

Mudflats

Estuary mud is thick and very smelly, but it is full of nutrients. This makes it a great home for animals such as worms and snails.

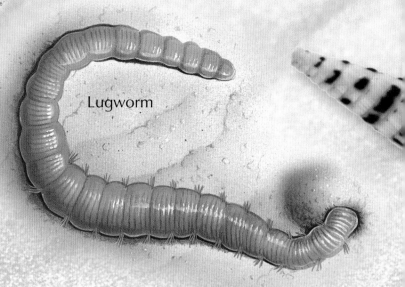

Lugworm

Long bills

Wading birds have differently shaped bills designed to help them feed. The oystercatcher, for example, uses its thick, straight bill to open the shells of mussels and razor shells.

Lugworm

The lugworm digs a burrow in the mud. It sucks water into its burrow and filters out any food. Wading birds prey upon lugworms, pulling them out of their burrows.

Oystercatcher

Snails

Mud is full of all kinds of snails, such as cockles, periwinkles, and spire shells. Spire shells are found on the surface, but cockles lie under the mud.

This snail has a spiral shell that protects its soft body.

Both eyes are on one side of the head.

Flounder

Flat fish

The bodies of flatfish such as plaice, turbot, and flounder are squashed from side to side. This shape is perfect for living on the seabed. If you look closely, you will see that one eye has moved so that both are on the top.

53

Marsh and swamp

Swamps and salt marshes lie close to the shoreline. When the tides are high enough, seawater often covers them, bringing in plenty of nutrients.

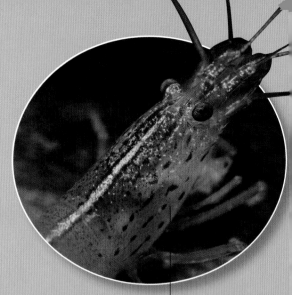

Young shrimp

Salt marshes

Salt marshes are formed when mud builds up behind banks of small stones, called shingle. Salt-loving plants, such as cord grass and sea lavender, start to grow. The marsh is crisscrossed with small streams, or creeks, that fill with salt water during high tides.

Nurseries

Salt marshes are breeding grounds for shrimp and fish. The young shrimp and fish spend the first part of their life in the safety of the creeks before they swim out to sea.

Marsh plants

Salt-marsh plants have to be able to live in salty ground. They are often covered by seawater. They have small, fleshy leaves that can store water. Samphire (right) is a plant that grows on salt marshes and can be eaten by humans.

Alligators

Alligators are reptiles. The American alligator is found in salt marshes and swamps, where it hunts mostly fish and crabs. Larger alligators attack deer, and even eat other smaller alligators.

Alligators have powerful jaws with many teeth that can crush bones.

Long, broad snout

Mangrove swamps

Mangrove swamps are found along tropical coasts near the equator. Here, there are strange-looking trees, fish that can walk, and crabs that wave to each other.

Swamp roots

Mangrove trees look as if they are growing on stilts because their roots, supporting them in the mud, come out of the water. The tangle of roots is a great hiding place for young fish.

Mudskippers

A mudskipper has gills, but it mostly breathes through its skin. This allows the fish to leave the water. It uses its stiff front fins to push its body across the mud and even up mangrove roots.

The tree roots come out of the mud.

DID YOU KNOW?

Mangrove swamps help to protect coasts from hurricane and tsunami damage. They act as barriers between the sea and the land.

Birds of prey

Ospreys are the top hunters in a mangrove swamp. They feed on fish and small animals. They build nests out of twigs, which they use for many years.

Fiddler crabs

The male fiddler crab has an extra-large claw that it waves up and down as a signal to other crabs. At low tide, male fiddler crabs sit at the entrance to their burrows and wave their claws to attract females.

Nesting on the beach

Many creatures, such as crabs and turtles, crawl onto beaches to lay their eggs. Their young hatch a few weeks later and hurry away to begin life in the ocean.

Digging a nest

Female turtles dig holes on the beach, where they lay about 100 eggs. They cover their eggs with sand and then return to the sea.

A green turtle uses its flippers to dig a nest hole in the sand.

Race for the sea

After baby turtles hatch, they dig their way out of the nest and dash across the sand to the sea. Birds and crocodiles gather on the beach to feed on the baby turtles as they emerge, but some make it safely into the ocean.

Horseshoe crabs

Each spring, when there is an especially high tide, up to one million horseshoe crabs appear on the beaches of Delaware Bay. Each female crab digs a small pit and lays about 20,000 eggs.

A thick, spiny shell protects the horseshoe crab from hunters.

A red crab's body is about 5 inches (13 cm) across.

Crab invasion

Red crabs live in the forests on Christmas Island in the Pacific Ocean. Once a year, the crabs leave the forests and walk to the ocean, where they breed on the beaches. In places, millions of crabs are on the move, covering the ground.

Coastal life

The shallow waters around land are full of life. Here, tiny plants called phytoplankton and animals called zooplankton float in the water. These plankton are food for large numbers of fish, which attract larger predators, such as sharks, whales, and seabirds.

Tiny plants

The moving ocean stirs up mud on the seabed. This releases nutrients into the water. These nutrients provide food for tiny plants called phytoplankton that float in the water.

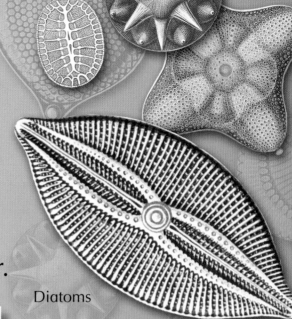
Diatoms

Phytoplankton (magnified x 50)

Diatoms

Diatoms are a type of phytoplankton that have hard, shell-like skeletons. The skeleton is in two parts, called valves, that fit together tightly. There are many types of diatoms, each with its own design of skeleton.

Phytoplankton

The phytoplankton form the bottom of the marine food chain. Just like plants on land, phytoplankton can make their own food using sunlight, carbon dioxide (a gas), and nutrients from the water.

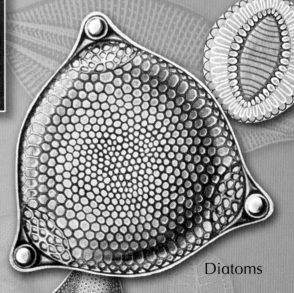
Diatoms

Dinoflagellates

Dinoflagellates make up much of the phytoplankton. At night, these tiny organisms give out a strange light. This is called bioluminescence.

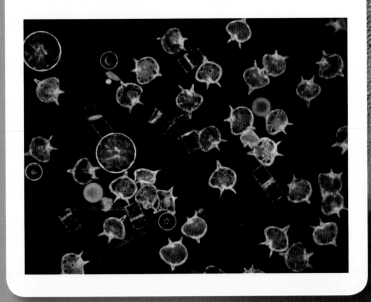

Plankton bloom

Sometimes, there are extra nutrients in the water and the phytoplankton increase in number. There are so many plankton that the water changes color. This is called a plankton bloom, and it can grow so large it can even be seen from space.

This large plankton bloom is off the coast of Argentina.

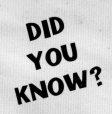

DID YOU KNOW?

Phytoplankton are able to grow and reproduce very quickly. They can triple in numbers in just one day.

Tiny animals

Phytoplankton are eaten by the creatures that make up the zooplankton, or animal plankton. These animals drift in the water, carried around by tides and currents.

Baby fish

Many fish lay their eggs in coastal waters. When they hatch, the baby fish feed on phytoplankton. They grow quickly until they are large enough to swim out to sea.

Microscopic creatures

Most animal plankton are tiny organisms, such as copepods and amphipods (above). The larvae (young) of marine animals such as starfish, jellyfish, and barnacles are also called animal plankton.

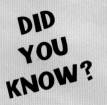
Jellyfish

Jellyfish are the largest type of animal plankton. They have a bell-shaped body and long tentacles, which hang below. Many just drift in the water, while others move by flapping their bell-shaped bodies.

Salps

Salps are tubelike organisms about the size of a large peanut. They suck in water and food. Where there is plenty of food there are large swarms of salps.

Salps may link together to form chains that are up to 16 feet (5 m) long.

Filter feeders

Most plankton feeders filter, or strain, tiny organisms from the water. Humpback whales (left) have frilly plates called baleen in their mouth that filter the water. Some other ocean creatures strain food from the water using their gills.

Plankton feeders

Animal and plant plankton are the favorite food of many animals, including ocean giants such as the blue whale, whale shark, and basking shark.

Big mouth

The basking shark swims along with its mouth wide open. When its mouth is full of water, the fish closes it and squeezes the water out through its gills. Any food is trapped inside by rakers (bristlelike filters) in the gills.

Manta ray

Most rays live on the seabed, hunting fish and small animals. The huge manta ray (left) is different. It is an active fish that swims great distances, filtering plankton through its gills.

Ocean wanderer

A whale shark's spots are unique and can be used to recognize each shark.

The whale shark is the largest fish in the world. It grows up to 43 feet (13 m) long and can weigh more than 22 tons (20 tonnes). It is a filter feeder and, despite its size, it is not a dangerous shark.

DID YOU KNOW?

Scientists believe that some whale sharks may live for up to 180 years.

Krill

Krill are among the most important animals in the ocean. There are billions of these small, shrimplike animals. They are eaten by whales, seals, penguins, and seabirds.

Krill

Living in numbers

Krill live in large groups called swarms. Up to 30,000 krill can be found in 35 cubic feet (1 cu m)—about four bathtubs—of water. The wriggling of the swarm confuses hunters.

Penguin predator

Krill are an important food for penguins. Chinstrap penguins (right) feed on larger types of krill, while Adélie penguins prefer the smaller ones. Penguins, together with whales, seals, and other seabirds, eat about 150–300 million tons of krill each year.

Raised on krill

Young leopard seals feed almost entirely on krill. As they get older, they eat larger fish. The adults are dangerous predators that hunt penguins, and even other seals.

The leopard seal filters krill from the water through its large, jagged teeth.

Squid

Squid swim through the water by pushing a jet of water out of their bodies. They catch krill using their long tentacles. Their sharp beaks rip the krill into small pieces for swallowing.

Squid

Holdfast

Seaweed

Seaweeds are found in shallow water close to the coast. They are not proper plants because they do not have leaves, stems, or roots, but they do make their own food.

Holding on

Seaweeds have sticky knobs, called holdfasts. These grip to the rocks to prevent the seaweed from being washed away by the tides.

Covering rocks

Many seaweeds are found on rocky shores. When they are covered by the tide, their leaflike fronds float in the water. When the tide goes out, they are left piled up on the rocks until the tide returns.

Oarweed (brown seaweed)   Dead man's fingers (green seaweed)   Bladder wrack (brown seaweed)

Types of seaweed

There are three main types of seaweed: green, brown, and red. Brown seaweed is the most common and is found on rocky beaches. Green seaweed is found only in shallow water.

DID YOU KNOW?

Seaweeds range in size from just a few inches to more than 200 feet (60 m) long.

Harvesting seaweed

People harvest seaweed from the sea. It is eaten as a vegetable in Japan and other countries. Seaweeds are also used as an ingredient in skin cream, shampoo, nail polish, ice cream, beer, paint, and as a fertilizer for soil.

Kelp forests

Kelp are large, brown seaweeds that grow closely together. Kelp forests, with their fronds gently moving in the water, are magical places where many animals live.

Thin leaves

Kelp have a stalk with long, thin leaves, called fronds, at the top. They are covered in a protective layer of mucus and feel tough, but are easily damaged in storms.

DID YOU KNOW?

There are different types of kelp. The giant kelp is the fastest growing of all. The length of its fronds can increase by up to 2 feet (60 cm) a day.

Dense growth

Kelp forests are found in shallow water, where they can get enough sunlight to make their food. At the surface, they form a thick, tangled mat.

Floating plant

A kelp has a small, balloonlike float at the bottom of the fronds. The float is full of air to keep the fronds floating near the water's surface, where there is more sunlight.

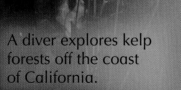

A diver explores kelp forests off the coast of California.

Kelp eater

Sea urchins eat kelp. In some places, there are too many sea urchins. They eat the young kelp before it has a chance to grow—so the forest disappears.

Kelp forest animals

More than 800 types of animal have been found living in kelp forests. There are shoals of brightly colored fish, feeding limpets, lurking blue sharks, and giant rays.

Forest hunter

The blue shark is a regular visitor to the kelp forest. It hides in the kelp waiting for prey, such as squid, to pass close by.

Blue shark

Eagle ray

The eagle ray (below) has huge winglike fins up to 6½ feet (2 m) wide. It turns on its side to swim between the stalks of the kelp.

Sea otter

Sea otters (right) feed on sea urchins and clams that they find in the kelp forests. Clams have hard shells, so otters collect stones, which they use to crack open the shells. They balance the stone on their stomach and hit the clam shell against it.

74

Garibaldi fish

The bright orange garibaldi fish aggressively defends its nest site in the kelp from all—including divers! The male builds a nest in which the female lays her eggs. He then looks after the eggs until they hatch.

DID YOU KNOW?

Sea otters sometimes wrap themselves in kelp. They use it as an anchor so that they do not drift away while they sleep.

Sea grass

There are underwater sea grass meadows along sheltered coasts. The sea grass shelters large numbers of fish and attracts animals, such as manatees and turtles.

Underwater grass

Sea grass gets its name from its grasslike appearance, but it is not a real grass. It is a plant that can grow, rooted in sand, in shallow sea water.

Manatee

The manatee, or sea cow, looks a little like a hippopotamus. It has paddlelike front legs to push itself through the water. It uses its large upper lip to graze the sea grass. An adult eats as much as 110 pounds (50 kg) of grass a day.

Sea horse

The sea horse swims upright in the water, using three small fins. It wraps its long tail around the sea grass so that it is not carried away on the currents.

A sea horse's long snout acts like a vacuum cleaner, sucking up tiny shrimp.

DID YOU KNOW?

Female sea horses lay their eggs inside a pouch in the male's belly. Four weeks later, he gives birth to up to 1,000 baby sea horses.

Lobster nursery

Sea grass meadows are nurseries for spiny lobsters. Adult lobsters come here to lay their eggs, which hatch into baby lobsters. When the lobsters are big enough, they move to nearby swamps and coral reefs.

Seabirds

The rich harvest of fish in coastal waters attracts a wide variety of seabirds, including pelicans, gulls, gannets, and cormorants. Seabirds can often be seen swooping down to the water in search of fish to eat.

Gannets

Gannets live in colonies on sea cliffs. They dive into the sea from a height of about 100 feet (30 m), and catch fish under the water using their pointed bills.

Pelicans

White pelicans often fish in groups. Together, they chase fish into shallow water, where it is easier to catch them. The pelicans scoop up the fish into a pouch under their bill, and then toss them down their throat.

DID YOU KNOW?

There are about 50,000 pairs of gannets nesting on Bass Rock, off the east coast of Scotland.

Gannets have long, narrow wings. The wings measure almost 6½ feet (2 m) from tip to tip.

Cormorants

A cormorant (left) can dive to depths of more than 130 feet (40 m), and then swim underwater using its large, webbed feet. Its hooked bill is perfect for gripping slippery fish.

Following whales

Seabirds such as gulls (right) gather around whales as they feed near the surface of the ocean. Whales drive a lot of fish and krill to the surface of the water, where the birds can reach them.

Baleen whales

Baleen whales are huge mammals that have comblike plates hanging from the roof of their mouth. They use these baleen plates to filter plankton and small fish from the water.

Baleen plates

A whale's baleen plates are made from keratin—like your fingernails are. The teeth of these plates are known as whalebones.

Whale's baleen plate

Blowholes

A blowhole is a whale's nostril, found on top of its head. Whales cannot breathe underwater, so they have to take a deep breath before they dive. When they return to the surface, air is forced from their lungs through the blowhole, which sprays water into the air.

Blue whale

Blue whale

At over 100 feet (30 m) long, the blue whale (right) is the world's largest animal. It eats about 7 tons (8 tonnes) of krill a day. It feeds at depths of 330 feet (100 m) during the day. At night, it follows the krill, which move to the surface to feed.

Grooves in this humpback whale's throat allow the throat to expand to four times its usual size when it is feeding.

Breaching

Whales sometimes leap out of the water and fall down with a big splash. This is called breaching. Scientists are unsure why they do this. It may be to signal to other whales, or it may be to remove parasites from their skin.

Toothed whales

Orcas, pilot whales, dolphins, and porpoises are toothed whales. Toothed whales usually live together in small groups called pods. They are hunters that feed mostly on fish and squid.

Arctic whales

The beluga whale (left) and narwhals live in the freezing waters of the Arctic Ocean. They have white skin, which is good camouflage against the ice.

Sharp teeth

Most toothed whales have small, cone-shaped teeth, which are perfect for gripping slippery fish. Orcas (killer whales) have about 50 teeth, but dolphins can have up to 100 teeth.

The dorsal fin on the back of a dolphin has a wavelike shape.

A pair of dolphins

Dolphin or porpoise?

Dolphins and porpoises look similar, but a dolphin has a pointed snout and a long, slim body. A porpoise has a rounded, fishlike snout and a shorter, rounder body.

Hunting seals

Some orcas living off the coast of South America have learned to surf onto beaches to catch sealions. The whales have to be careful not to become stranded on the beach.

Coastal nurseries

Many animals visit coastal waters to breed or to have their young. These shallow waters are often sheltered, and there is plenty of food for the young animals.

Hammerhead gathering

Each year, hammerhead sharks gather together in special breeding places. Each male selects a female, and they mate. After about 10 months, the female swims into shallow water to give birth to her pups.

Hammerhead sharks gathering to breed.

Laying eggs

Many squid live in shallow water close to rocks, caves, and sea grass. The female lays eggs with short stalks, which she attaches to rocks and seaweeds so that they do not get carried away by the tides.

Squid eggs

Underwater flier

Manta rays live in the deep sea but give birth in shallow coastal waters, where the young stay for several years. The females are pregnant for about a year before giving birth to one or two pups.

Manta ray

Whale migration

Many whales make regular journeys along the world's coasts. Humpback whales spend the summer in cold waters, where there is plenty of food. They then migrate, or travel, to warmer, shallow water, where the females give birth.

DID YOU KNOW?

The yearly migration of gray whales from Baja, California, to the Arctic and back is a distance of 12,500 miles (20,000 km)—the longest journey made by any mammal.

Coral reefs

Coral reefs are some of the most colorful places on the planet. They are found in shallow, tropical waters and are home to thousands of different creatures. Only the surface of the coral reef is living.

Where in the world?

Coral reefs are found in warm seas, where the water is shallow and there is plenty of light. Coral will grow only in clean water that is free from pollution.

Reefs around the world

Most coral reefs are found in the Indian and Pacific Oceans, the Caribbean, and the Red Sea. Corals are not found where there are cold ocean currents or where large rivers flow into the sea.

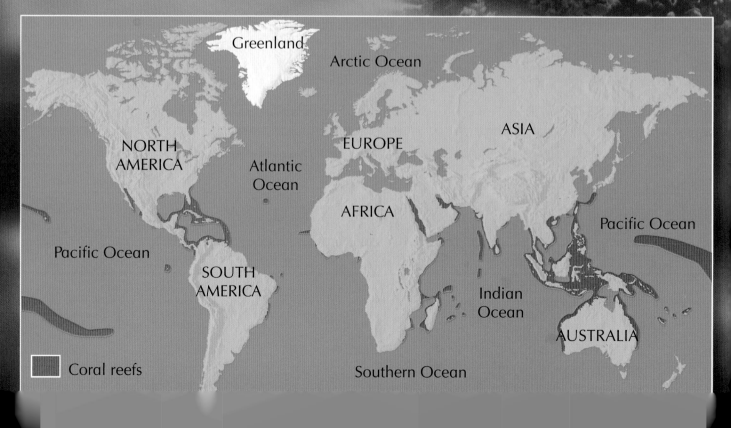

Greenland

Arctic Ocean

NORTH AMERICA

Atlantic Ocean

EUROPE

ASIA

AFRICA

Pacific Ocean

Pacific Ocean

SOUTH AMERICA

Indian Ocean

AUSTRALIA

Coral reefs

Southern Ocean

Bathed in sunlight

Corals need sunlight because they have tiny algae, called zooxanthellae, in their cells. These algae use the sunlight to make their own food. The algae also provide the corals with food and, in return, they get shelter and protection.

Exposed coral

Some coral reefs close to the shore are exposed when the tide goes out. The exposed coral is then damaged by the sun and wind.

Great Barrier Reef

The Great Barrier Reef is the world's largest coral reef. It runs along the northeast coast of Australia and is 1,500 miles (2,500 km) long. Almost 6,000 species of animals live on it.

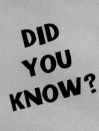

DID YOU KNOW? The Great Barrier Reef is the largest structure made by living creatures on Earth. It is so large that it can be seen from space.

Polyps

Tiny builders

Reefs are made by a group of tiny coral animals living together. Each tiny coral animal is called a polyp. A polyp (left) has a tubelike body and a ring of tentacles around its mouth.

Living reef

Coral reefs are built by hard corals (see pages 94–95). These are coral animals that leave behind stony skeletons when they die. Their skeletons create a habitat in which other animals can live.

Feather star

Feather stars (below) are related to starfish and live on the coral reef. They have a cup-shaped body and many feathery arms. The arms are covered in a sticky substance that traps small animals as they float by.

Feather star

Living in crevices

Many animals, such as the moray eel (right), hide in the cracks and crevices on the reef. The moray eel darts out and grabs any small fish that swim too close.

Sponges

Sponges are animals, but they do not move around. Some sponges grow to 6½ feet (2 m) tall. Others form a flat, crustlike growth over the surface of the reef.

Vase sponges

DID YOU KNOW?

There are more than 5,000 different types of sponge. Some of the largest may be hundreds of years old.

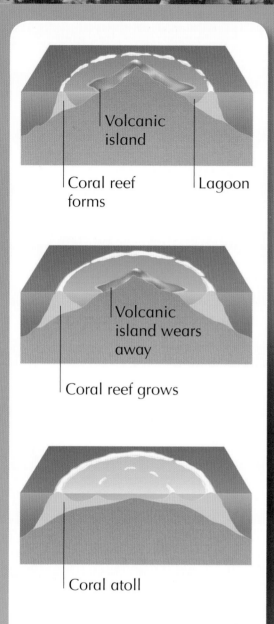

Volcanic island

Coral reef forms

Lagoon

Volcanic island wears away

Coral reef grows

Coral atoll

How an atoll forms

Atolls take millions of years to form. Volcanoes create islands in the oceans. Then coral animals build reefs around the islands. Over a long time, the volcanic islands wear away but the reefs keep growing, leaving behind the atoll rings.

Types of reef

There are three types of reef. A fringing reef is formed by corals that follow a coastline, while a barrier reef grows farther away from the land. An atoll is a circular reef around an area of shallow water, called a lagoon.

Coral atolls

A coral atoll (above) protects the lagoon inside from the ocean waves. Most of the world's atolls are found in the Indian and Pacific Oceans.

New coral growing on a wrecked ship.

New coral

Coral polyps like to grow on something hard. They will even make their home on the remains of a sunken ship.

Coral sand

Waves batter against the coral reef, and the reef gradually wears away. The tiny particles of reef are washed up on the shore as sand, eventually creating beautiful tropical beaches.

DID YOU KNOW?

The largest atoll in the world is Kirimati, or Christmas Island, in the Indian Ocean. Around 1,500 people live on the atoll. They even have their own flag and postage stamps.

A beach with fine coral sand

Hard corals

Hard corals are those with limestone skeletons. There are many different species of hard coral, each forming an interesting shape on the reef.

Table coral

Table coral (below) is a fast-growing, spreading coral that forms a flat, tablelike shape. It grows to several feet across and is made up of lots of short branches.

Brain coral

Brain coral (above) gets its name from the way it looks like the folded surface of a real brain. These corals grow up to 6 feet (1.8 m) tall, and are strong enough to survive in rough seas.

Mushroom coral

The mushroom coral (right) is round or oval in shape. It can be flat or domed and is about 20 inches (50 cm) across. Most corals are made up of many polyps, but this type has just one large one.

Black coral

Black corals (right) are found in deeper water, where there is less light. They are branching corals, which look a little like bushes with small branches. The skeleton is black but the polyps are white, yellow, or orange.

Soft corals

Soft corals come in a wide range of colors, such as red, yellow, orange, and purple. Soft corals are those that do not have a hard skeleton.

Feeding corals

Coral polyps feed by extending their tentacles into the water to catch small animals. The tentacles are covered in stinging cells, which they use to kill their prey and to defend themselves.

Yellow finger gorgonian coral

Underwater fans

Fan corals (above) form lovely fan shapes up to 10 feet (3 m) across, which move gently in the currents. Each fan has a flexible stem attaching it to the rocks.

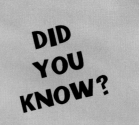

DID YOU KNOW?

Soft coral is known as a flower animal because of the many different shapes and colors it can take on.

Whip coral

Whip corals (below) look
a little like long drinking
straws. They bend in the
ocean currents, catching
plankton to eat, but do
not get damaged.

Fire coral

Fire corals have a powerful sting.
This protects the polyps from coral-eating
fish. Fire corals are often found on the edge
of the reef, and can survive in rough water.

Clown fish

Living together

Animals live closely together on the reef. Some depend on others for a home, to stay clean, or for protection from predators.

Living with stings

Anemones are covered in sting cells. Most animals stay away, but not the clown fish. It lives in the safety of the tentacles—it is covered with a slimy mucus that protects it from the stings.

Living camouflage

The hermit crab protects its soft body by living inside an empty shell. Anemones have attached themselves to this hermit crab's shell (left). The anemones provide the crab with camouflage and protection and, in return, the crab helps the anemones to find food.

Cleaning station

Fish have difficulty removing the tiny parasites that live on their bodies, so they visit "cleaning stations." Here, small fish and cleaner shrimp remove, and eat, the parasites for them.

Wash and brush up

The moray eel (below) opens its mouth so that the cleaner shrimp can remove parasites from every nook and cranny.

Kissing sturgeon

Wrasse

DID YOU KNOW?

Decorator crabs attach sponges and seaweeds to their shell. These living decorations help to disguise the crab from predators.

Eating coral

Coral is an important source of food for many reef animals, including turtles, starfish, snails, and a lot of fish.

Fish with beaks

The parrot fish uses its large, beaklike teeth to bite off lumps of coral covered in algae, crunching them into small pieces. Much of the coral passes through its gut and ends up as sand on a beach!

Hawksbill turtle

This turtle (right) has a pointed beak. It is perfect for reaching into crevices on the reef to find sponges, which are its favorite food.

The parrot fish gets its name from the teeth at the front of its mouth, which look like a parrot's beak.

Butterfly fish

Butterfly fish (above) have a flat body and a long, thin snout. They are the perfect shape to pick out small animals from inside coral crevices. Butterfly fish are brightly colored with beautiful patterns— just like butterflies!

DID YOU KNOW?

In one year, a crown-of-thorns starfish can eat up to 140 square feet (13 sq m) of coral.

Reef devourer

The large crown-of-thorns starfish (right) has a huge appetite for coral. It has up to 18 arms and is covered with poisonous spines. At night, it crawls onto coral and empties its stomach contents. The digestive juices turn the coral into a liquid, which the starfish then sucks up.

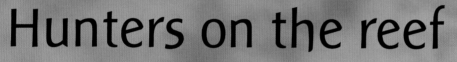

Hunters on the reef

The thousands of fish and small animals living on the reef attract a lot of predators. These include barracuda, octopuses, and lion fish.

Barracuda

The barracuda (above) has powerful jaws, knifelike teeth, and a long body. It hangs without moving in the water, then darts forward to grab prey with a burst of speed.

Lizard fish

The lizard fish sits on the reef propped up on its front fins with its head raised. It darts forward to catch prey, such as small fish.

Lion fish

This is a
dangerous
fish—its spines
are tipped with
poison. Lion fish trap prey
using their large, spiny fins—
and then swallow it whole.

Reef octopus

The reef octopus hides in holes with
just its legs sticking out. It grabs its
prey of fish or clams with its suckers
and pulls it toward its mouth.
The octopus then uses its powerful
beak to crush its meal.

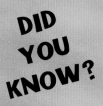

**DID
YOU
KNOW?**

Young barracudas
live in large shoals
consisting of
thousands of fish.

Reef sharks

Sharks are among the most feared animals on the reef. Large reef sharks cruise along the reef edge looking for fish, while smaller sharks hunt shrimp and crabs among the corals.

Blacktip reef shark

Underwater zebra

Adult zebra sharks (right) have spots, but when they are young they have stripes, just like a zebra. Their downward-pointing mouth is designed to feed on clams from the seabed. They also hunt crabs and small fish.

White-tipped reef shark

The white-tipped reef shark is brownish gray in color, but has white tips on its fins. It rests during the day, and hunts for food at night in the crevices of the coral reef.

A white-tipped reef shark resting under a coral ledge.

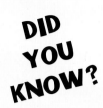

DID YOU KNOW?

There have been only two attacks ever recorded on scuba divers by blacktip reef sharks.

Blacktip reef shark

Blacktip sharks are the top predators on the reef because they are not hunted by other animals. This shark hunts in shallow water and lagoons. It catches sea snakes as well as fish and octopuses.

Laying eggs

Some types of shark lay eggs. Each egg is protected inside a tough case. Curly threads fix the case to seaweed so that it is not swept away by the waves. The egg case of the dogfish shark (right) is called a mermaid's purse.

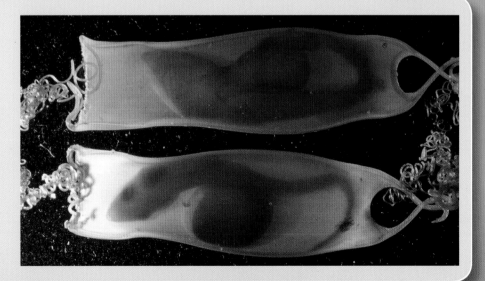

Reef defense

Reef animals protect themselves from predators in different ways. Some use body armor or poisons to defend themselves. Others rely on camouflage to keep them hidden on the reef.

Body armor

Sea horses use body armor to defend themselves. The tough armor gives them good protection, but makes swimming more difficult. They stay still much of the time, relying on their camouflage to hide them from hungry hunters.

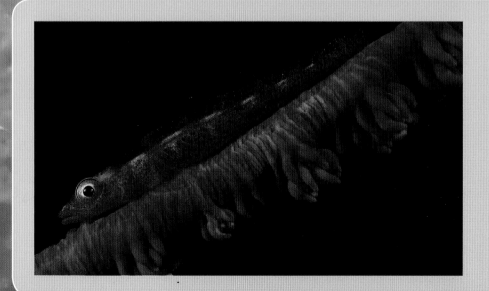

Hiding in coral

Corals make great hiding places for the creatures that live on them. Tiny animals, such as this small goby (left), hide from their predators on and among the coral branches.

Frog camouflage

Frog fish (above) look more like a piece of coral or sponge than a fish. By keeping perfectly still, they blend in with the reef and are difficult for predators to spot.

Spiny defense

The cowfish's spiky body armor, with long spines over each eye, gives it an unusual appearance. If the cowfish is attacked, it can also release a poison into the water from its skin.

Out at night

The reef is active at night because many of the animals are nocturnal. They hide in caves and crevices during the day, then come out to feed in the safety of the dark.

Cardinal fish

The female cardinal fish lays her eggs in the water, where they are fertilized by the male. The male then collects the eggs in his mouth and cares for them until they hatch. He releases the young fish in the safety of darkness.

Cardinal fish

Nighttime crab

The arrow crab is a nighttime scavenger. It clambers over coral looking for the remains of animals that have died on the reef.

The arrow crab has eight spiderlike legs and two legs that end in claws.

Safety in numbers

Snappers (above) are seen at night swimming around in small groups. They hunt crabs, shrimp, worms, and fish that live on sandy seabeds near reefs.

Squirrel fish

Squirrel fish have very large eyes. These fish hide in caves and wrecked ships by day, and come out at night to feed on plankton.

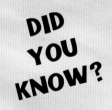

DID YOU KNOW?

Cardinal fish carry their eggs around in their mouth for 18 to 24 days before the young fish hatch.

Reef mollusks

Mollusks are a group of animals that include snails, clams, and squid. Most mollusks have a muscular "foot," which they use to move around.

Shell protection

A heavy shell, such as this helmet shell, protects the soft body of a snail. When threatened, the snail retreats into its shell. This is a spiral shell, but some are cone shaped.

Giant clam

The giant clam is a bivalve—a snail with two shells that are hinged together. Clams stay in one place on the reef, sucking water into their body and filtering out plankton. Their color comes from algae that live in their cells and provide the clams with food.

Nudibranch

Nudibranches are soft-bodied sea slugs that have no shell. Without a shell for protection, they use poison to protect themselves from predators. Nudibranches are brightly colored to warn other animals that they are poisonous.

Coming out to play

These flamingo tongue snails (right) are coral eaters. As they crawl over the coral, their feet release digestive juices. The juices dissolve the polyps, and the snails absorb the nutrients through their feet.

DID YOU KNOW?

The largest giant clams grow to more than 3 feet (1 m) across, weigh more than 440 pounds (200 kg), and can live for up to 100 years.

Open oceans

Stretching beyond the coastal water is the vast, open ocean. It covers thousands of miles and extends down for thousands of feet. The open ocean looks empty at first glance, but there are many different kinds of animal living beneath the surface. These range from tiny microscopic creatures to whales—the largest animals that have ever lived on the planet.

Surface waters

The open oceans are home to fewer animals than coral reefs and coastal waters. Most animals that do live here are found in the surface layer, which is the top 655 feet (200 m).

Light in the water

The ocean's surface is lit by sunlight. The top 100 feet (30 m) are brightly lit, but it gets darker deeper down. By 655 feet (200 m), all sunlight has gone and the water looks bluey black.

Flying fish

The flying fish has an unusual way of escaping predators. When threatened, it swims straight at the surface of the water and flies into the air, using its fins like wings. It can glide above the surface for up to 330 feet (100 m).

Surface waves

When the wind blows over the surface of the ocean it creates waves. As the waves grow larger they are moved along by the wind, and this helps to mix up the water.

The wind pushes along wind-powered boats, such as this yacht.

Humpback whales

Whales, such as these humpback whales, have to come to the surface of the ocean to breathe. Most whales swim near the surface and dive deeper only to find food.

DID YOU KNOW?

During storms at sea, it is not unusual for waves to reach more than 100 feet (30 m) in height. That is as tall as a 10-storey building!

Floating life

The surface layer is home to many floating animals, both large and small. These are carried across the ocean by the currents and waves.

Floating stings

The Portuguese man-of-war (left) looks like a jellyfish (see pages 118–19), but it is a colony of individual polyps called a siphonophore. One polyp floats above the surface to catch the wind, while others form hanging tentacles to trap food.

Comb jellies

Comb jellies look like jellyfish without any tentacles. The body is just a few inches long. When comb jellies catch the light, they shimmer in rainbow colors.

116

Siphonophores

Like all siphonophores, this deep-water species (right) is formed from a colony of individuals—each with a different job to do. Its long, stinging tentacles dangle in the water to catch fish and shrimp.

Tiny squid

The larvae of squid and fish are found in the surface layer, where they drift in the currents. These tiny larvae hunt even smaller animals, such as copepods and amphipods.

These squid larvae use their short tentacles to catch small animals.

DID YOU KNOW?

The world's longest animal is a species of siphonophore. It can grow to more than 130 feet (40 m) long.

Jellyfish

Jellyfish are not actually fish. They are invertebrates with a jellylike body, and are related to corals and sea anemones.

Floating bells

Jellyfish have a soft, bell-shaped body with tentacles hanging beneath the bell. Each tentacle is covered in cells that can sting or kill other creatures.

This jellyfish has tentacles covered in stinging cells.

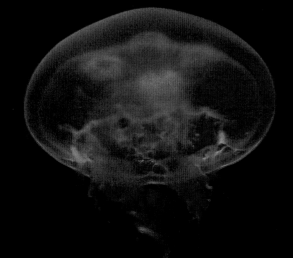

Underwater moons

Most jellyfish float in the water and are carried around by currents. Some can swim very slowly by squeezing water in and out of their bell—which looks a little like an umbrella opening and closing.

Lion's mane

The largest jellyfish is the lion's mane. Its bell is more than 3 feet (1 m) across and the tentacles are many feet long. They eat almost anything that bumps into their tentacles.

Sea nettles

Sea nettles (below) are a small type of jellyfish. Each year, in some parts of the world, swarms of sea nettles gather to lay eggs. Sea nettles can sting, so people and marine animals stay away from these areas.

DID YOU KNOW? Each year, more people are killed by jellyfish than by the more feared great white shark.

Shoals of fish

Many fish live together
in groups called shoals.
Some shoals contain just
a few fish but, when shoals
join together, a huge shoal
of hundreds of thousands
of fish may form.

Living in groups

Fish are safer in large groups.
A shoal of fish confuses hunters
by darting around in different
directions. The fish use their senses
to make sure that they do not bump
into each other.

A shoal of mullet leaps
out of the water to
escape a dolphin.

A shoal of fish
moves away from an
approaching diver.

Jumping to escape

When a group of dolphins finds
a shoal, they surround it and then
chase the fish. Some fish leap out
of the water to try to escape.

Bigeye jacks

These fish are powerful hunters with large eyes and a forked tail. They patrol the oceans in large shoals seeking out smaller fish, which they catch in their large jaws.

DID YOU KNOW?

During the 1970s, enormous herring shoals of more than three billion fish were thought to exist in the North Atlantic Ocean.

Huge shoals

Sardines (right) form huge shoals. These attract hunters such as dolphins, sharks, and swordfish. Sardines are an important link in ocean food chains (see pages 26–27).

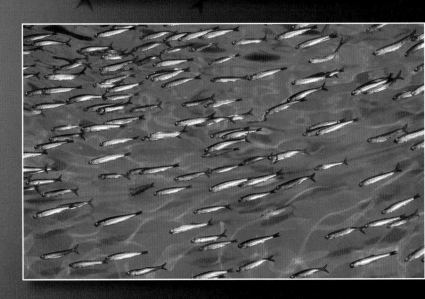

Catching fish

Fish are an important part of our diet. Each year, large fishing boats called trawlers catch millions of tons of fish.

Trawling the seas

People living along the coast have always fished the seas. Over time, the size of the fishing boats and their nets have increased. Modern trawlers stay at sea for longer and use the latest equipment to find fish.

Various fish

Thousands of different types of fish are regularly caught around the world, but only about 20 types are fished in large quantities. These fish fall into five groups—cod, herring, jacks, mackerel, and redfish.

This beam trawler has two nets. Each net is kept open by a bar, or beam.

Trawler nets

The type of net used by a trawler depends on the type of fish being caught. A beam trawler is used to catch fish on the seabed, and a purse seine (right) is used to catch a shoal of fish. Purse seining involves dropping a long net around the fish then closing the net from the bottom, trapping the fish. Tuna are caught using a long line of hooks.

Cod under threat

The cod is one of the most important fish in the Atlantic. An adult fish grows up to 55 inches (1.4 m) long and weighs up to 55 pounds (25 kg). The cod's survival is under threat because it has been overfished (see pages 192–193). In some oceans it is classed as endangered.

DID YOU KNOW? There are about four million fishing boats in the world. Each year, they catch about 80 million tons (90 million tonnes) of fish.

Nets of the beam trawler are lowered to the seabed.

123

Squid

Squid is an important link in the ocean food chain. It is a hunter of smaller animals, such as krill and fish, and is itself the prey of hunters such as swordfish and dolphins.

Jet propulsion

To move along, a squid draws water into its body and then forces it out through a funnel on its belly. This creates a powerful jet of water that pushes the squid backward through the water.

Large squid can move at 19 miles (30 km) per hour—faster than many ships can travel.

This squid has caught a fish in its tentacles.

Tentacles

A squid has eight arms and two tentacles. When it gets close to its prey, it shoots out its long tentacles to grab the animal and pull it into its mouth.

Small suckers cover the underside of the tentacles.

Colorful messages

Squid can change the color of their skin. They can blend into the background or change color to confuse a predator. Their color reflects their mood, too. Angry squid are often red. This squid (left) is bioluminescent—it gives off an eerie glow in the dark.

Large eye

Squid have large eyes that are very similar to human eyes, with a pupil and a lens. They rely on their sight to find prey.

DID YOU KNOW?

Squid can die if they become stranded in shallow water. This often happens after they mate and lay their eggs.

Ocean hunters

Large hunting fish such as sharks, swordfish, and marlin are at the top of the food chain. These fearsome fish are perfectly designed for hunting.

The dorsal fin forms a crest along the back of the fish.

Marlin

The marlin (right) is related to the tuna and swordfish. It is a large fish with a spearlike snout. It hunts alone, swimming in the surface waters of the ocean in search of fish and squid.

Swordfish

The swordfish (above) is named after its long, swordlike snout. It does not spear its prey, but moves its "sword" from side to side to slice it up. It swims alone and is often seen leaping out of the water.

Sailfish

These fish have a large, sail-like fin along their back. They use it to herd together groups of fish and squid, which are their prey. Sailfish can fold back the fin to create a sleek, streamlined shape for swimming.

DID YOU KNOW?

Sailfish are the fastest swimming fish. They have an amazing top speed of 68 miles (110 km) per hour.

Mako shark

The mako is a muscular fish with a tail fin shaped for speed. It can swim at up to 20 miles (32 km) an hour. It has sharp teeth, which it uses to grip slippery prey such as tuna and mackerel.

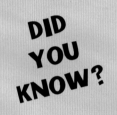

Giant fish

Some creatures found in the oceans are huge. These include whales and fish such as basking sharks, disk-shaped sunfish, and winged manta rays.

Manta ray

A manta ray (right) usually swims slowly through the ocean, but when threatened by hunters, such as sharks, it leaps out of the water in an attempt to escape.

The wings of a manta ray can be up to 23 feet (7 m) wide.

Ocean-going shark

The white-tipped shark grows to about 13 feet (4 m) long. It usually swims slowly just below the surface, but sometimes sticks its nose out of the water to sniff the air in search of food.

Wahoo

The wahoo (above) can grow up to 5½ feet (1.7 m) long. It is nicknamed the "striped rocket" because of the shape of its body, and its habit of leaping out of the water with its prey in its jaws.

DID YOU KNOW?

The average length of a sunfish is 6 feet (1.8 m), but some have been found that are 10 feet (3.2 m) long.

Sunfish

The sunfish has an unusual shape—it is almost circular when seen from the side, with fins sticking out of the top and bottom of its body. It can weigh more than 4,400 pounds (2,000 kg). Sunfish feed mainly on jellyfish.

Ocean turtles

Many turtles make long journeys across the oceans in search of food. They return to the beach where they were born to lay their eggs.

Growing up

Turtles spend the first few years of their life in the open ocean. They feed on jellyfish and other animals there, before returning to coastal waters to mate.

Green turtle

Turtles have flat flippers to help them swim.

Green turtles

Green turtles are expert swimmers with a smooth, streamlined shell. They are the largest hard-shelled turtle in the ocean. They grow up to 3 feet (1 m) across, and can weigh 440 pounds (200 kg) or more. Baby green turtles eat sea grass, but the adults are meat eaters.

Hawksbill turtles

This rare turtle gets its name from the birdlike shape of its head. It spends up to 20 years at sea before it is ready to breed. Sadly, it is killed for its attractive shell, which is used to make jewelry and ornaments.

Toothless turtles

All turtles are toothless. Instead of teeth they use their beak to crush coral and crabs, or graze on sea grass. Their head, like the rest of their body, is covered with small scales.

Toothless beak of a hawksbill turtle

DID YOU KNOW?

Some green turtles feed off the coast of Brazil and swim across the Atlantic to breed on Ascension Island—a round journey of about 2,800 miles (4,500 km).

131

Dolphins

The dolphin is one of the most intelligent animals in the ocean. This playful marine mammal uses sound to find its prey and lives in groups.

The bottlenose dolphin can spin in the air before landing back in the water.

Leaping dolphins

The acrobatic dolphin moves its powerful tail up and down to build up enough speed to jump out of the water. Dolphins often leap into the air while chasing fish to eat.

Hunting with sound

Dolphins use sound to find their prey. This is called echolocation. They make whistling and clicking sounds, which travel through the water. These sounds bounce off any prey in the water, creating echoes that the dolphins can hear.

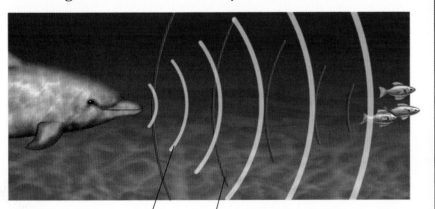

Sound waves made by dolphin.

Echoes tell the dolphin the shape, size, and location of its prey.

Looking after baby

A female dolphin gives birth to her calf, or baby, under the water. The mother pushes her calf to the surface so it can take its first breath. The calf feeds on its mother's milk for about a year.

Living together

Dolphins live together in groups called pods. A pod usually contains 10 to 12 dolphins, but super pods of thousands of dolphins are formed when pods join up.

Sargasso Sea

The Sargasso Sea is a huge area of floating seaweed in the North Atlantic Ocean. It is home to many animals—some stay all year, but others are just visitors.

Small air sacs keep the sargassum weed afloat.

Sargassum weed

Thick mats of sargassum weed cover much of the Sargasso Sea. Turtles and fish hide among the mats, while crabs and small shrimp cling to the weed.

NORTH AMERICA

EUROPE

Atlantic Ocean

Sargasso Sea

AFRICA

SOUTH AMERICA

In the mid Atlantic

The Sargasso Sea covers an area of about 1 million square miles (3 million sq km). It is an area of water with slow currents surrounded by a boundary of fast-moving currents.

Seaweed nurseries

The Sargasso Sea is a nursery for many fish. The young of the gray trigger fish (above) drift in the sargassum weed until they reach about 6 inches (15 cm) long. Then they swim to coastal reefs.

Growing eels

Adult eels swim to the Sargasso Sea to lay their eggs. The young eels hatch then slowly make their journey back to North America and Europe, where they swim up rivers to breed.

DID YOU KNOW?

The vast Sargasso Sea is the only sea in the world that does not have a coastline. Instead it is bordered by fast-moving water.

Young eels

Moving up and down

During the day, the brightly lit surface waters are virtually empty of small animals. Many dive to the safety of the darker water below. At night, it is very different—they all return to feed under the cover of darkness.

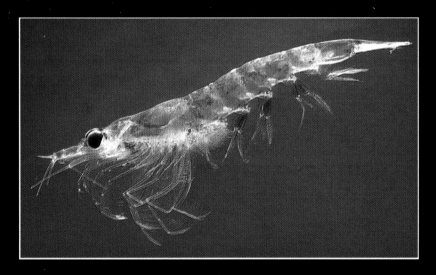

Nighttime travelers

This daily movement is only a few hundred feet, but for tiny animals, such as shrimp (left) and copepods, it is a long journey. It is the only way to feed in safety.

Mass migration

During the day, most animals living in the open oceans are found at depths of 165 to 3,300 feet (50 to 1,000 m). At sunset, they swim back to the surface waters. This is one of the largest mass movements of animals in the world.

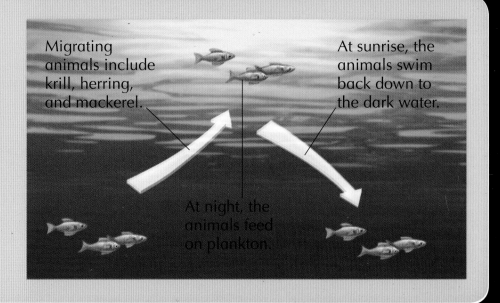

Migrating animals include krill, herring, and mackerel.

At sunrise, the animals swim back down to the dark water.

At night, the animals feed on plankton.

Lantern fish

Lantern fish travel the greatest distances each day. During daylight, they are found more than 5,600 feet (1,700 m) down, and at night they rise to within 330 feet (100 m) of the surface.

DID YOU KNOW?

Lantern fish get their name from the rows of glowing lights along their body. These lights are bioluminescent organs called photophores.

Bluefin tuna

The tuna preys on smaller fish, which it swallows whole. It follows its prey on their migration to the deeper water.

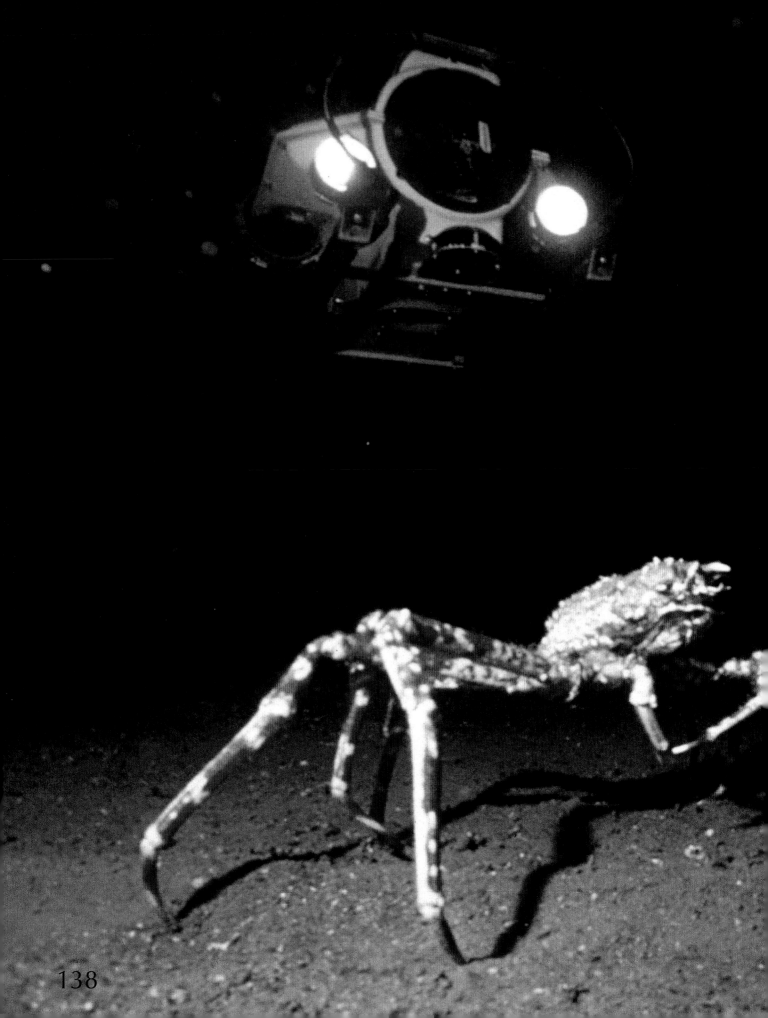

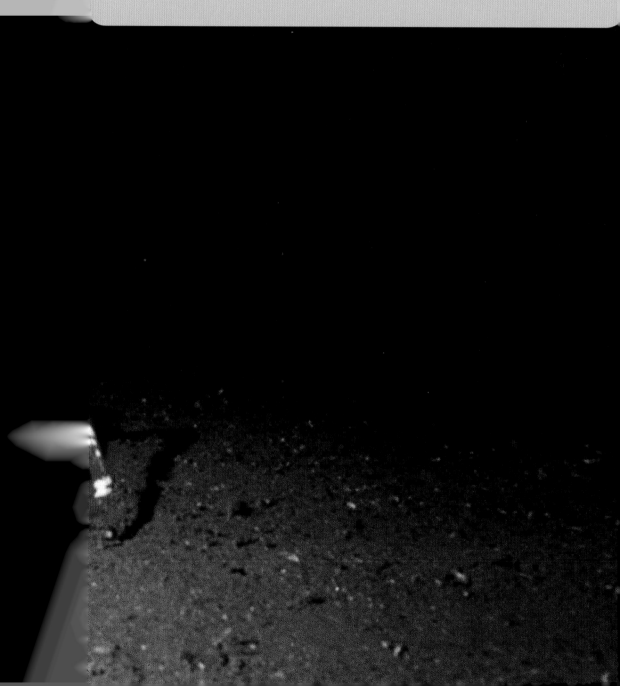

The deep ocean

People have explored the land and the surface of the oceans, but the deep ocean is still mysterious. This dark, cold place is the world's largest habitat, but few people have ventured into it. The deep ocean is a difficult place for animals to live in—and for humans to visit.

Ocean layers

The surface layer extends to 660 feet (200 m). Next comes the twilight zone, from 660 to 3,300 feet (200 to 1,000 m). The dark zone reaches down to the seabed.

Going down

As you descend from the surface, the sea becomes darker and colder. The pressure increases, too. In very deep water, a diver would be crushed and all the air squeezed from his or her lungs. Only animals adapted to this environment can survive.

Sunlit zone

Sunlight passes through the water to about 660 feet (200 m) deep. Here, in the surface layer, there is enough light for plant plankton and seaweeds to make their food.

Twilight zone

Beneath the surface layer there is a glimmer of light—just enough for some animals to see. Visiting animals dive down into this layer for safety.

Dolphins spend most of their time in the sunny surface layers.

The sperm whale is an expert diver. It spends hours in the dark zone searching for food.

Brittle stars are found crawling over the seabed.

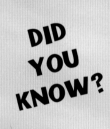

Dark zone

The dark zone is pitch black and cold, and the water is still. Fish and other sea creatures living at these depths are designed to cope with the great pressure of the water.

Twilight zone

A variety of animals, from tiny plankton to huge whales, live in the twilight zone. Their bodies are specially adapted for life in deep, gloomy water.

Hatchetfish

A hatchetfish (above) has a flat body. It has light-producing organs on its underside. The lights disguise the fish's shape so it is not spotted by predators in the water below.

Nautilus

The nautilus is a relative of the squid. It has a spiral shell for protection and, if necessary, it can pull itself right inside. Its large eyes help it to see in the gloom.

The nautilus has many more tentacles than a squid, but no suckers.

Eye

Twilight shrimp

The twilight shrimp (right) has a red shell—a color that is difficult to spot in the gloom. It catches small plankton animals in its claws.

Fangs in the dark

There is not much food in the twilight zone, so fish make sure that any prey they catch cannot escape. Fish such as this fangtooth have daggerlike teeth that point backward. This prevents their prey from wriggling out of their mouth.

Diving deep

Seals, whales, sharks, and penguins are just some of the animals that dive down into the twilight zone and beyond to find food.

Twilight hunter

The sperm whale dives down to 3,300 feet (1,000 m) or more in search of squid. Scientists believe that the whale produces sound waves to stun its prey.

Diving birds

Many seabirds, such as the penguin, dive underwater to catch food. The penguin is a flightless bird with flippers instead of wings. It is clumsy on land, but an expert swimmer. The emperor penguin spends up to 15 minutes under the water at a time. It dives to depths of around 1,600 feet (500 m).

A sperm whale wrestling with its prey of giant squid.

Weddell seals

The Weddell seal dives at night to find krill, squid, and fish. It can stay under the water for up to an hour, reaching depths of about 2,300 feet (700 m) before it has to return to the surface to breathe.

Megamouth

The odd-looking megamouth shark grows to about 23 feet (7 m). It has a 3-foot (1-m)-wide mouth and a flabby body. Like many ocean animals, it spends the daylight hours in deep water and swims to the surface to feed at night.

DID YOU KNOW?

Little is known about the megamouth shark, which was first discovered near Hawaii in 1976. Since then, only about 40 megamouths have been seen.

The snipe eel has a row of small backward-facing teeth along its jaws.

The deep

The deep is a cold, eerie place where very little lives. The animals of the deep have all sorts of unusual features, which help them get something to eat in this "food desert".

Snipe eel

The snipe eel has jaws that do not close. It swims with its mouth open, and small animals such as amphipods (shrimplike creatures) are trapped on the teeth and swallowed. The snipe eel grows to over 3 feet (1 m) long.

Deep-sea medusa

The deep-sea medusa (right) is a relative of the jellyfish. It traps prey, such as small shrimp and baby fish, in its long, stinging tentacles.

The gulper eel has a loosely hinged jaw, which can open very wide.

Big mouth

Many deep-sea fish are all mouth and stomach. The gulper eel has a wide mouth and a very stretchy stomach—it can swallow prey as large as itself.

Fishing the deep

The anglerfish lures its prey with a light that dangles from the end of a spine in front of its large mouth. The light is produced by tiny bacteria.

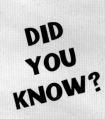

DID YOU KNOW?

It is believed that the *phronima*, a tiny amphipod, was the model for the monster in the science-fiction film *Alien*.

Deep-sea squid

Many stories have been written about monsters of the deep. One of the most mysterious is the giant squid. These huge animals are very rare, and few have been seen alive.

Historical monster

Many stories have been written about giant squid. In these tales, it is said that they have risen from the deep and wrapped their tentacles around boats to pull them down under the water.

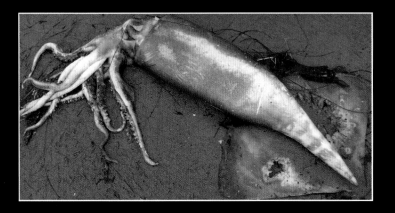

Rare sightings

Sometimes, the bodies of giant squid (above) are washed up on beaches. This gives scientists the chance to study them. Their remains have also been found in the stomachs of sperm whales.

Light in the dark

Many giant squid (below) can produce their own light. They switch this light on and off to attract fish. When the fish are close enough, the squid grab on them.

This deep-sea squid, called *Teuthowenia*, produces its own light to attract prey.

DID YOU KNOW?

The colossal squid has the largest eyes of any animal. Each eye measures up to about 10 inches (25 cm) across.

Colossal squid

The colossal squid is even larger than the giant squid. It is the world's largest invertebrate animal, reaching a massive 46 feet (14 m) in length. Its tentacles have razorlike hooks, which can cause injuries to other animals.

Life on the seabed

Some of the deep seabed is rocky, but it is mostly covered by a thick layer of mud. This mud contains the remains of dead animals that have sunk from the water above.

Deep-sea spines

The round sea urchin is covered in long spines. Its mouth is on the underside, surrounded by five teethlike plates. It uses these plates to feed on dead matter and animals such as mussels and sponges.

The sea urchin can move each of its spines.

Sea pens

Sea pens (above) are related to corals. Each sea pen is really a colony of individual polyps that live together. The sea pen attaches to the deep seabed, where it catches small animals with its stinging tentacles.

Sea slug

The sea slug (above) is a mollusk with a tube-shaped body, leathery skin, and a ring of sticky tentacles around its mouth. It uses its tentacles to find food in the mud.

Long-legged crabs

Spider crabs scuttle across the deep seabed in search of food. They have a small body and 10 very long legs. They cannot see anything in the dark, so they use their sense of touch to catch prey.

Spider crabs use their claws to feel for food in the mud.

All kinds of worms

Worms are invertebrate animals with a long, soft boneless body. There are all kinds of deep-sea marine worms, including fan worms and tapeworms.

Spaghetti worm

The tentacles of this deep-sea worm (right) look a little like spaghetti. The worm extends these sticky tentacles over the seabed to catch any small particles that sink down from above.

Hook

Tapeworms use their hooks and suckers to grip to the inside of the gut.

Undersea parasites

Parasites are animals that live in, and do harm to, other animals. The tapeworm is a common parasite in many deep-sea fish. It lives and feeds in the fish's gut. Eventually, the fish starves to death.

Sucker

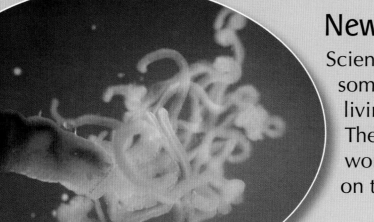

New discovery

Scientists have discovered some new types of worm living on the deep seabed. These include a type of fan worm (left) that feeds only on the bones of dead whales.

Catching food

Fan worms are found on the deep seabed. Their soft body is protected by a hard, bony tube. They extend a ring of sticky tentacles from the top of the tube to catch small animals drifting in the water. If disturbed, fan worms can shoot back inside their tube.

DID YOU KNOW?

More than 400 different species, or types, of animal, including many worms, feed on the bodies of dead whales on the seabed.

153

Food and shelter

When the body of a large animal drops to the seabed, scavengers come from far and wide to feed upon it. Others find shelter among anything that finds its way to the seabed.

Finding shelter

Animals on the seabed need shelter from predators. Many hide among bones, or even old cans (below) and other garbage that has sunk to the seabed.

Food from above

There is a constant supply of "marine snow" from the waters above. This "snow" is the broken down remains of dead plants and animals— especially plankton. These remains sink slowly to the seabed.

Ocean floor scavenger

The hagfish (above) looks a little like an eel. It is a scavenger that burrows into the bodies of dead animals, and eats them from the inside out. It is an unusual fish because it does not have jaws or teeth. Instead, it has a very rough tongue.

Brittle star

The brittle star (right) has five long arms, which it uses to pull itself across the seabed. It sometimes preys on small shrimp and other animals, but mostly scavenges on dead matter.

Starfish

The spiny skin gives protection from predators.

There are hundreds of tube feet on the underside of each ray.

Starfish

Starfish are spiny-skinned creatures that belong to a group of animals called echinoderms. They are related to sea urchins, sea cucumbers, seastars, and brittle stars.

Sunstar

All arms and legs

Most starfish and sunstars have five or more arms, called rays, which are joined to a central body. The mouth is on the underside. Starfish pour acid from their stomach onto their food. The acid dissolves the food so the starfish can digest it.

Starfish

Tube feet

To move, a starfish swings each ray forward then pushes down, pulling itself along. There is a tiny sucker at the end of each ray, to grip. The starfish also uses the sucker to force open the shells of mussels and clams.

Spare parts

If a starfish loses one of its rays, it can grow a new one. This process is called regeneration. This starfish (below) is regrowing two of its rays.

Mouth

Sea lilies

Sea lilies, or feather stars, are related to starfish. They have a central mouth surrounded by arms. Some sea lilies attach to the seabed by a stalk, but others can swim.

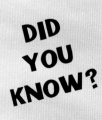

DID YOU KNOW?

Sea lilies have survived, almost unchanged, for millions of years. Fossilized sea lilies have been found that are up to 130 feet (40 m) wide.

Seabed fish

A surprising number of fish are found on the deep seabed, and more are being discovered all the time. They have been given unusual names, such as the rat-tail, cookie cutter, and even the blobfish.

Deep-sea blob

The blobfish (below) was discovered in 2003, on a seabed 3,900 feet (1,200 m) deep. Little is known about it, but the shape of its mouth suggests that it eats whatever it can find.

Six-gill shark

The six-gill shark (above right) is found at depths of up to 10,000 feet (3,000 m), where it rests during the day. At night, it swims to the surface to hunt for fish and seals. Most sharks have five gill slits, but this shark has six.

Gill slits

Cookie cutter shark

This shark gets its name from the round scars that it leaves on its prey. It grips its prey in its mouth and, using its long teeth, pulls out a lump of flesh, leaving behind a nasty hole.

DID YOU KNOW?

The cookie cutter shark has a dark patch on its belly. This fools hunting fish into thinking it is a small fish. It waits for them to attack, and then it turns on them!

Deep-sea rat-tail

The rat-tail, or grenadier, is one of the most common deep-sea fish. It has a large head and a slender body and, unusually, no tail fin. These fish live in water up to 16,000 feet (5,000 m) deep, and hunt animals, such as smaller fish and shrimp.

Cliff hugger

Sea anemones, and other animals that cannot swim, cling tightly to the cliffs. If they let go, they could sink into the deep below.

A deep-sea crab hides underneath an anemone on a sea cliff.

Deep-ocean cliffs

There are cliffs, mountains, and trenches in the deep ocean. These are home to many animals, including corals and sponges.

Deep-sea glass sponge

Glass skeleton

Deep-sea sponges

Some deep-water sponges have a skeleton that is made from glass. They produce tiny pieces of glass, which stick together to form a beautiful skeleton that is strong enough to support their body.

Deep-sea coral

More corals live in cold, deep water than on shallow coral reefs. Some live 3,300 feet (1,000 m) deep. Deep-sea reefs grow slowly, and some are hundreds of years old.

Hiding in cracks

The wolf fish, or seawolf, pushes its body backward into the cracks of a cliff. It leaves just its head sticking out, watching for prey. It has a wide mouth with large, pointed teeth, which it uses to feed on clams, mussels, and starfish.

Strange new life

In 1976, scientists made an exciting discovery while exploring the deep. They found strange animals, never seen before, clustered around jets of hot water coming out of cracks in the seabed.

Jet of black water

Deep-sea smokers

The jets of water are often nicknamed black smokers. The temperature of the water reaches 750°F (400°C). A chimney builds up around the jet, formed from minerals in the hot water.

A chimney can reach 200 feet (60 m) tall, and can grow up to 1 foot (30 cm) a day.

DID YOU KNOW?

In the Atlantic Ocean massive swarms containing up to 30,000 shrimp per square yard have been found near or on black smokers.

Tube shrimp

Each chimney is home to a single type of shrimp. The shrimp feed on bacteria, and in turn are eaten by crabs and fish.

Deep sea mussel

Black smoker

Tube shellfish

Mussel larvae are often the first animals to settle beside a smoker chimney. The mussels move by sending out a sticky thread, which attaches to the rocks, and they pull themselves along.

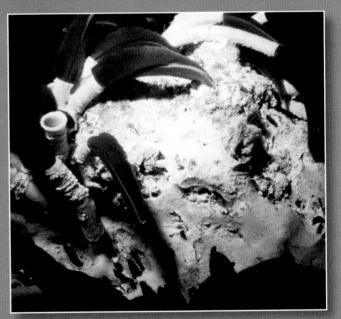

Mussels

Tube worms

Giant tube worms

Giant tube worms can grow to more than 6½ feet (2 m) in length. They do not have a mouth, so cannot feed. Their food comes from bacteria that live inside them.

Polar waters

Animals living in the polar regions have to cope with some of the toughest conditions on the planet. The Arctic Ocean surrounds the North Pole. At the South Pole, the continent of Antarctica is covered by a thick sheet of ice. The Southern Ocean surrounds Antarctica, and is also covered by ice for much of the year.

Polar climate

The poles have winters of freezing temperatures, high winds, and darkness. In summer, temperatures rise and it stays light all day and all night.

Arctic

Antarctica

Ice caps

These maps (left) show the area that is covered by ice all year round. In winter, the areas of ice are even larger.

Blizzard conditions

Strong polar winds blow snow into the air, creating blizzards. This makes it difficult for animals to move around. Emperor penguins huddle together for shelter.

A colony of emperor penguins in a blizzard in Antarctica.

166

Midnight sun

At midnight during the polar summer the sun does not set. There is enough light to see 24 hours a day. In the winter, the sun does not rise, so it is dark all the time.

This series of photographs of the Arctic summer sun was taken during the night. It shows that the sun never sinks below the horizon.

Lights in the sky

During spring and fall, strange lights of red, blue, and green appear in the polar skies. This display is called the aurora borealis in the Arctic. In the Antarctic it is the aurora australis.

DID YOU KNOW? At the North and South Poles there is only one full sunrise (where the whole sun can be seen) and one full sunset (where the whole sun disappears) each year.

Sea ice

The surfaces of the polar oceans are covered by ice during the winter. As temperatures fall, the sea water freezes, forming a thick layer of ice called an ice sheet.

Sheets of ice

Fresh water freezes at 32°F (0°C), but the salt water of the polar oceans freezes at 28.5°F (−2°C). The thick sheet of ice formed at the surface is not flat. Strong winds push the sheets of ice together to form ridges.

Life under the ice

Sea ice forms a protective layer, beneath which live many animals. These include Arctic cod and smaller animals, such as krill and copepods. These animals attract hungry predators, such as seals (above).

Growing on ice

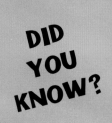

Sea ice is not solid like a block of ice. It is crisscrossed with small channels filled with salty water. Tiny living things, such as algae (left), bacteria, and copepods live in these channels. Sometimes there are so many red algae that the ice looks red.

Breaking up ice

In spring, when temperatures rise, the ice sheet breaks up into large chunks called floes. These get smaller and smaller as they are moved around by the ocean currents.

DID YOU KNOW?

The Arctic is the least salty ocean in the world. This is because the lack of warm sunshine means that less water evaporates than elsewhere.

Many polar animals, such as seals and penguins, pull themselves out of the water onto the sea ice to rest.

Icebergs

Icebergs are huge, floating lumps of ice that have broken off ice sheets. They are carried across oceans by winds and currents.

Under the water

Only about one eighth of an iceberg sticks up above the water (left). The rest is hidden under the water. Icebergs are a danger to ships because sailors cannot see the massive lumps of ice lurking beneath the surface.

Massive icebergs

In 2005, a huge iceberg broke off the Antarctic ice sheet. It was 75 miles (120 km) long—the largest floating object in the world. It is now blocking the way to the ocean for penguins. This is a problem for the penguins because they have to walk farther over the ice to reach the water to feed.

The large iceberg is stuck across a bay.

Ocean

Ice islands

Icebergs look clean and white, but they are often covered with a layer of dirt. They can contain rocks, soil, and parts of plants. Each year, as many as 40,000 icebergs break off ice sheets in the Arctic. Most drift south into the Atlantic Ocean, where they slowly melt.

Sunk by an iceberg

On April 14, 1912, a ship called the *Titanic* sank after hitting a huge iceberg in the Atlantic Ocean. The *Titanic* was on its first voyage and was the world's largest ship at the time. Of its passengers, 1,500 people died and 700 were rescued by other ships.

An iceberg tore a hole in the *Titanic*.

The wreck of the *Titanic* was discovered in 1985.

Living on ice

Animals that live at the poles are adapted to cope with the cold, wind, and snow. These include polar bears, Arctic foxes, and walruses.

Prowling the ice

The biggest hunters on the ice are the polar bears (left). Their long claws and furry feet help them to grip the slippery Arctic surface.

Polar scavenger

Arctic foxes are scavengers, so they eat almost anything they find on the ice. They also hunt small animals. When Arctic foxes hear small rodents, such as voles or lemmings, under the snow, they pounce on them from above. They often bury food to eat later.

The pads of the Arctic fox's feet are covered with thick fur.

Thick insulation

Most polar animals, such as the walrus (right), have a thick layer of fat under their skin to keep them warm. Walruses need the insulation for swimming in the icy water of the Arctic.

Walruses have two tusks, which are extra-long teeth. ———————

Giving birth on ice

Seals spend much of their life in water hunting for food. Female seals move onto the ice each year to give birth to their young, called pups.

DID YOU KNOW?

If a walrus gets too hot, it turns pink. This is because its blood flows closer to the surface of its skin to lose heat. This helps to cool the walrus down.

Under the ice

The polar ice spreads over much of the Arctic and Southern Oceans. Many animals spend their lives under the ice.

Southern fish

Ice fish live in the deep, cold waters around Antarctica, where they feed on krill and plankton. They grow slowly and live for up to 20 years. Ice fish are caught to be eaten but, sadly, too many have been taken from the ocean and they are now rare.

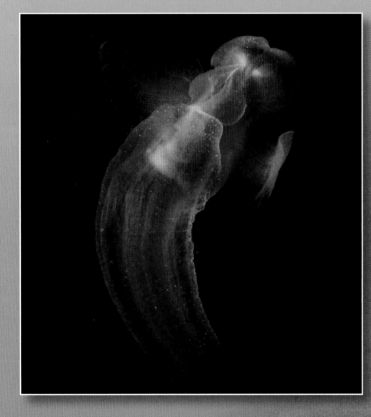

The ice fish is so-called because it looks as though it is made of ice.

Sea butterfly

The sea butterfly (above) is a type of mollusk without a shell. It has two wings, or flaps, attached to its body, which it uses to move through the water. It feeds on copepods and plankton.

DID YOU KNOW?

Ice fish live in such cold water that they have a special chemical in their blood to stop water from freezing in their body.

Arctic jellyfish

Scientists exploring under the ice have discovered new forms of marine life, including Arctic jellyfish. These large jellyfish feed on plankton and small fish.

This Arctic jellyfish has long tentacles, which can extend up to 20 feet (6 m).

Arctic cod

Arctic cod like icy water, and are not often seen in warmer water. They grow to 1 foot (30 cm) long, and are the favorite food of narwhals and other Arctic whales.

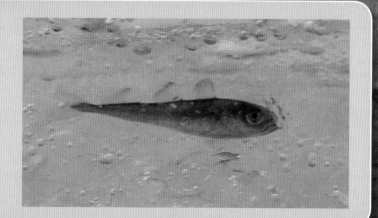

Penguins

Penguins are birds that do not fly. They are found mostly in the Antarctic and the surrounding islands of the Southern Ocean, where they spend many months at sea.

Graceful swimmers

Penguins are good swimmers, with a sleek, streamlined body. They use their paddlelike wings to push through the water. They press their feet against their tail, which they use to steer.

Penguin colonies

Each year, penguins come together to breed. Like seals, they gather in colonies. These groups vary in size from a few hundred breeding pairs to hundreds of thousands of birds.

A colony of emperor penguins

Leaping penguins

Penguins waddle and slide across the ice to the sea before leaping into the water. If they are chased by predators in the water, they swim quickly then leap back onto the safety of the ice.

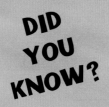

Bringing up baby

Both parents look after a chick, taking it in turns to walk to the sea to catch fish. The parent bird stores fish in its stomach, and brings it back up into its mouth to feed the chick.

A chinstrap penguin feeding a chick.

Seals

Seals are built to live in polar waters. They have a streamlined body, flippers to help them swim, and a thick layer of fat, called blubber, to keep them warm.

Crabeater seals

There are more crabeater seals (right) in the world than any other seal. There may be as many as 50 million. Despite their name, they do not eat crabs—they feed on krill. Their main predators are leopard seals.

Seal pups

Seal pups are born on the ice. They feed on their mother's milk, which is high in fat, so that they grow very quickly. A harp seal pup can gain as much as 4½ pounds (2 kg) in weight each day.

The white fur of this harp seal pup will change to gray within a few weeks.

Walruses

Walruses are easily recognized by their two long tusks. They are noisy animals, making a wide range of sounds—such as growls, barks, grunts, and clicks—both when they are under the water and above it.

Coming up for air

Ringed seals (left) can stay under the water for up to 30 minutes, but they have to come to the surface to breathe. When the water starts to freeze over, the seals make breathing holes in the ice, which they keep open throughout the winter.

DID YOU KNOW?

Hungry polar bears sit next to breathing holes in the ice, waiting for a seal to pop out its head.

Polar whales

Most whales, including the humpback, visit polar waters only to feed. But some whales, such as belugas, spend all year in the chilly Arctic.

White whale

The beluga (left) is a white whale found in the Arctic. It is very noisy and talks to other belugas using a range of sounds, including whistles and squeaks.

Polar unicorns

Male narwhals have an unusual spiral tusk. The tusk is actually a very long tooth. These whales (right) are rubbing their tusks together. This is not aggression, but a way of communicating with each other.

Looking for prey

The massive killer whale, or orca (below), hunts in polar waters, feeding on animals such as fish, squid, penguins, and seals. Orcas often hunt together—when they see penguins or seals resting on a small ice floe, one orca tips over the ice while the others wait to catch the prey.

The orca is easy to recognize by its black and white markings.

Trapped by ice

In winter, ice extends quickly over the water and whales that are feeding in bays or between large floes can get trapped. They die if their breathing holes in the ice close up.

DID YOU KNOW?

In 1978, five humpback whales and one narwhal were trapped by ice in a bay in Newfoundland, Canada. For two months, people kept breathing holes open for the whales until the ice melted and they could escape.

Polar bears

Polar bears are the largest hunters of the Arctic. Their white fur is good camouflage against the white snow. Their excellent senses help them to find prey on the ice.

Polar hunter

Polar bears are at the top of the Arctic food chains. They have few enemies other than people. They feed mainly on seals, but also eat birds, fish, and mammals.

Polar bears paddle with their front paws and steer with their hind legs.

Champion swimmer

Polar bears are strong swimmers and can swim huge distances. They often have to swim between ice floes as the ice starts to break up in spring.

Scavenging

A dead whale washed up on a beach provides a feast for polar bears. Polar bears live alone, but large numbers will gather each day to feed on a dead whale.

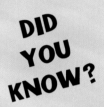

Polar cubs

Female polar bears usually give birth to two cubs. In winter, the mother lives in a den under the ice and snow, where her cubs are born. In the spring, mother and cubs emerge to find food.

183

Albatrosses

Albatrosses spend much of their lives at sea, gliding over the Southern and Pacific Oceans in search of fish.

Gliding over the waves

The long wings of the albatross are the perfect shape for catching the wind and gliding. Albatrosses cover huge distances—some types fly more than 620 miles (1,000 km) in just one day.

The wandering albatross has the largest wingspan of any bird, reaching to 11½ feet (3.5 m). Each wing is almost as long as an adult human being is tall.

Polar nests

Most albatrosses breed once every two years. They return to land to nest on rocky cliffs and coastal slopes. The females lay a single egg, which hatches several months later.

Albatross chicks

Both parents care for the albatross chick, feeding it with fish and squid for up to seven months. An albatross is ready to breed when it is about 10 years old, and lives up to 60 years.

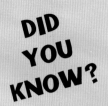
Hook bill

An albatross's bill is up to 7 inches (18 cm) long, with a hook at the end. The bird swoops down to the surface of the water and catches slippery fish and squid in its large bill.

185

Arctic tern

Speedy fliers

Arctic terns fly farther than any other birds. They spend half of the year in the Arctic, where they lay their eggs and raise young. The parent birds and all their young then fly south to the Antarctic for rest of the year.

Summer visitors

Arctic winters are harsh, but long summer days attract a lot of animals. Birds spend the summer here feeding and raising their young. In fall, they fly away to warmer places.

Greylag geese

Greylag geese (left) are large geese with gray-brown feathers and pink legs. They are so-called because they lag behind other birds and are often the last geese to fly north in spring.

Snow geese

Flocks of snow geese (above) fly north each spring. They leave their winter feeding grounds in the United States to return to the Arctic. Snow geese are white with black wing tips.

Whooper swan

Whooper swans

Whooper swans breed in Northern Europe and Iceland. Individual birds can be identified from the black markings on the bill, because each bird has different markings.

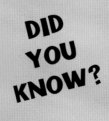

DID YOU KNOW?

Arctic terns live for about 20 years and will fly about 500,000 miles (800,000 km) in their lifetime. That is farther than flying to the moon and back.

Living and working at the poles

Some people have lived in the Arctic for many generations and others, such as scientists, have moved there to work. The only people who live in the Antarctic are scientists.

Surviving on ice

Hunters spend many weeks on the Arctic ice hunting for food. They build a domed shelter, called an igloo (above), from blocks of ice. It is warm inside the igloo, because the ice traps a person's body heat.

Traditional life

In the past, native people such as the Inuit (left) relied on the sea for their food and on animal skins to make their clothes. They cut up and dried fish so it could be eaten all winter when it was not possible to fish in the frozen sea.

Polar fishing

The polar waters are full of fish. Throughout the summer months, when the ice melts, many fishing boats sail into the region. They catch fish, squid, and shellfish such as crabs and shrimp.

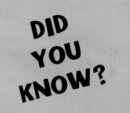

DID YOU KNOW?

About 4,000 scientists live in the Antarctic during the summer. However, fewer than 1,000 spend the long, cold winter there.

Studying polar life

Many scientists are based in the Arctic and Antarctic, studying the animals and the polar environment. These scientists (right) have caught and tagged a Weddell seal so they can track its movements.

189

Oceans in danger

People use the oceans to transport goods around the world, as a source of food, and even as a dumping ground for all kinds of waste. Sadly, people are damaging the world's oceans. This damage is caused by overfishing, pollution, and global warming.

Overfishing

Fish is an important source of food for many people. As the world's population grows, more fish, squid, shrimp, and other seafoods are being caught.

Hauling in the nets

Trawlers drag huge nets that can catch tons of fish at a time. "Purse seine" nets are designed to trap whole shoals. Long lines of hooks catch thousands of fish at the surface or on the seabed.

Fishing fleet

These fishing boats, called trawlers, use modern equipment to find shoals of fish. However, large trawlers use a lot of energy. It takes twice as much fuel to catch a ton of fish as it did 20 years ago. This is because fish stocks are lower, and boats have to travel farther to find them.

Fish sticks

Some fish are processed onboard. The fish are cleaned, gutted, and boned leaving a piece of fish meat called a fillet. This can be sold as fresh fish, or made into processed foods such as fish sticks.

Overfishing using trawlers such as this disrupts ocean food chains—they do not leave behind enough fish for marine animals to eat.

DID YOU KNOW?

Fishing nets that are dragged along the seabed cause a lot of damage to deep-sea coral reefs and other marine habitats.

Catching sharks

Sharks are caught for their meat and fins, which are used in shark fin soup. Often, the fins are cut off and the sharks are thrown back into the water, where they die. Sharks grow slowly and do not reproduce quickly. Too many are being caught and some species may die out.

Farming fish

Fish have been farmed in some parts of the world for thousands of years. Farming fish can help to save the world's wild fish, but only if it is done carefully.

Feeding fish

Farmed fish are fed a diet containing all the nutrients they need for healthy growth. The fish grow quickly and, when they are the right size, they are taken to market.

A worker feeds salmon at a fish farm in Maine.

A salmon farm in Scotland

Salmon farms

Salmon are raised in large, floating cages (above) along the coasts of countries such as Scotland and Norway. The salmon can swim about in the cages, but they cannot escape.

Trout farming

Trout are also raised on fish farms. There can be problems with farmed fish. The fish may become diseased and have to be treated with chemicals, which can cause pollution.

Salmon

Trout

194

A shrimp pond
in Thailand

Shrimp ponds

Shrimp farming is common along tropical coastlines. Mangrove swamps are cleared to make way for shrimp farms. This upsets the local food chain, endangering plants and animals.

A cooked shrimp

DID YOU KNOW? Each year, salmon farms around the world produce more than a million tons of fish.

Fish conservation

Overfishing means that too many fish are being taken from the world's oceans. There are several ways in which people can fish that protect future stocks.

Protected breeds

One way to protect fish is to ban fishing in areas where endangered fish species breed. This gives young fish a chance to survive to adulthood so that they can breed.

Fishing bans

When fishermen started using "purse seine" nets, they caught whole shoals of herring. Fishing in the North Sea was banned for a while to allow herring stocks to recover, but there are still not as many as there used to be.

Fish markets

There are good stocks of some types of fish, such as pollock. People can help to protect fish by choosing to eat those that are plentiful instead of those that are dying out.

Checking nets

Fishermen can use nets with larger holes, so that smaller, younger fish can escape and only the larger, older fish are caught.

A fishermen checking a net.

Ocean transport

Ships of all kinds carry people and goods around the world. Huge container ships carry goods, tankers are full of oil, and cruise ships have thousands of passengers onboard.

Propeller dangers

Sometimes, marine animals and boats crash into each other. Animals can be seriously hurt by the propeller blades at the back of a boat. Many manatees (right), for example, have been harmed by tourist boats getting too close.

Sonar confusion

Some scientists believe that booming sounds produced by submarines can confuse marine mammals, such as whales and dolphins. It may cause the animals to swim into shallow water and become stranded on beaches.

A manatee inspects a propeller off the coast of Florida.

Shipwreck

Sometimes, cargo ships sink during storms or after collisions and their load falls into the sea. The *MS Napoli* (right) broke up off the south coast of England in 2007. Its containers were washed up onto nearby beaches.

Containers from the *Napoli* washed up on the coast of southern England.

Oil spills

Tankers transport millions of tons of oil across the world's oceans. There have been many accidents involving oil tankers, where spilled oil ends up in the water.

Tanker wreck

In 1993, the *Braer* was stranded in water off the coast of Scotland. The wind and waves carried oil along the coast and onto nearby beaches.

Cleaning the shore

It is difficult to clean an oily beach. Tractors are needed to dig up the oily sand, and rocks have to be pressure-cleaned with powerful jets of water. Sometimes it is better to let the oil break down naturally.

Oil pours out of the *Braer* tanker, onto the surface of the water.

Wildlife under threat

Any bird, mammal, fish, or other animal that swims into an oil slick gets covered in the thick oil. It sticks to the birds' feathers and animals' fur, and blocks fishes' gills. Many die right away, but a few may be rescued.

Helping animals

Birds try to clean the oil off their feathers and end up swallowing it. Oily birds are taken to rescue centers, where they are cleaned and cared for until they are well enough to be released.

DID YOU KNOW?

One of the worst oil spills happened in 1989, when the *Exxon Valdez* leaked 10 million tons of oil into the sea around Alaska. Up to 500,000 birds, 5,000 sea otters, 250 bald eagles, and many salmon, whales, and seals died.

Dumping ground

Over the years, people have dumped a lot of waste, such as garbage, chemicals, and sewage, in the world's oceans. Tides carry the waste out of sight, but it still harms marine animals.

Killing fish

Fish need clean water full of oxygen so they can breathe. Fish living in coastal waters can be harmed by sewage, fertilizers, and chemicals emptied into the sea. Extra nutrients caused by sewage and fertilizers can increase bacteria growth. This uses up all the oxygen in the water, so the fish die.

Polluting sewage

Millions of quarts of sewage (left) is emptied into the oceans each year. Some of it is treated, but a lot is raw. Raw sewage smells horrible when it washes back onto beaches. It also contains harmful bacteria that cause disease.

Garbage hazards

Garbage often sinks to the seabed, where ocean creatures can be entangled. It also washes up on beaches, where it can harm birds and animals.

Waste by sea

Many countries have strict rules about the ways in which garbage is dealt with on land. The rules for dumping waste from ships (above) far out at sea are less strict.

DID YOU KNOW?

Cruise ships create 1,300 gallons (5,000 liters) of sewage and 7,900 gallons (30,000 liters) of waste water a day! Raw sewage can be dumped in the sea if the ship is at least 12 miles (19 km) from land.

Dangers to animals

A garbage-clearing boat in France

Each year, hundreds of thousands of animals die because of garbage in the oceans. Some die after eating the garbage, while others are trapped in old fishing nets and lines.

Cleaning up

The tides wash garbage onto beaches all around the world. Recently, volunteers found more than 370,000 pieces of litter on 116 miles (187 km) of British beaches. Boats are used in some places to scoop garbage out of the sea before it washes ashore.

Floating garbage

Floating plastic bags can look a little like jellyfish and are eaten by dolphins, whales, and turtles. The bags can block animals' guts and cause them to starve and die.

A spinner dolphin playing with a plastic bag.

Killer nets

Some of the largest fishing nets are many miles long. They hang like curtains in the ocean. As well as fish, the nets catch dolphins, whales, sharks, and turtles. These animals become tangled in the nets and may die.

Freeing trapped animals

Divers around the world help to save trapped animals such as turtles, dolphins, and even whales. They cut them free from the nets so they can swim away.

A diver frees a turtle that was trapped in a shrimp net.

Freed turtle

DID YOU KNOW?

In 2002, a minke whale was found dead on a beach in France. It had 1,750 pounds (800 kg) of plastic bags in its stomach.

Whaling

Many species of whale are protected today, but this has not always been the case. For hundreds of years, people hunted whales for their meat and oil, and some species almost died out.

Whaling today

In 1986, some countries agreed to ban whaling. It was decided, however, that some native people could still hunt and kill whales, and that some could be killed for scientific reasons. Countries such as Japan and Iceland want to start whale hunting again.

A picture of whaling ships from the 1800s.

Whaling in the past

There was a huge increase in whaling in the 1840s. People used a weapon called a harpoon to kill the whales. More than 40,000 whales were caught each year. By the 1970s, there were fewer than 6,000 whales left.

Whaling protests

Many people think whaling is wrong, and organizations such as Greenpeace lead protests against it. Greenpeace boats (right) try to stop whaling boats from catching whales.

Herding whales

Each year, the people of the Faroe Islands carry out a pilot whale hunt. They drive the whales into bays, using boats, and kill them in shallow water. Some local people eat the meat and say the hunt is part of their culture. Others want it stopped.

Dead whales lie on a beach in the Faroe Islands.

A dead whale is dragged ashore in the Madeira Islands in 1972, before whale hunting was banned.

DID YOU KNOW?

Since the ban in 1986, almost 27,300 whales have been killed. Many of these have been killed by Japanese whaling boats—for scientific purposes.

Whale shark

Changing habits

As the sea gets warmer, some marine animals change their behavior. They appear in places where they have not been seen before. As coral reefs die (see pages 210–211), some sharks may have to look elsewhere for food.

Global warming

Global warming is the gradual increase in the temperature of the Earth's surface. Scientists believe this will cause climates to change, sea levels to rise, and extreme weather to become more common.

DID YOU KNOW?

As oceans warm up, ice melts, the water expands, and sea levels rise. Sea levels have increased by as much as 10 inches (25 cm) in the last 100 years.

Smaller hunting grounds

Warmer weather is causing the Arctic ice to melt earlier each year. This causes problems for polar bears (right). The bears hunt on the ice and, if it melts, they are not able to catch enough food and may starve.

Polar bears

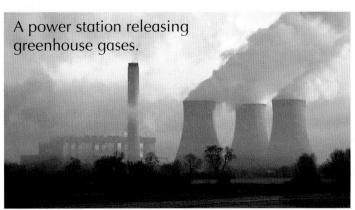

A power station releasing greenhouse gases.

Polluting the atmosphere

Global warming is thought to be caused by an increase in greenhouse gases, such as carbon dioxide. These gases trap heat in the atmosphere. Carbon dioxide is produced when oil, gas, and coal are burned.

How we can help

Everybody can help to slow down global warming by walking and cycling, which does not burn oil. If we travel in cars, buses, or airplanes, more carbon dioxide is produced, which may increase global warming.

Saving coral reefs

Coral reefs are fragile habitats that are easily damaged. They are under threat from global warming, water pollution, and overfishing.

Killing coral

Corals like warm seas but, if the temperature increases, the organisms living in the corals leave and the corals turn white and die (below). This is called bleaching.

A motorcycle on the wreck of
SS Thistlegorm in the Red Sea.

Creating new reefs

Shipwrecks are soon covered in
corals and other reef animals.
New reefs can be created
by sinking old ships, cars,
and tanks in warm,
shallow water.

Clearing reefs

Like beaches, coral reefs can
also become covered in garbage.
Divers can help to conserve the
reefs by removing plastic bags, glass
bottles, cans, and other garbage.

Making a new home

This squirrel fish (below) is hiding in a
pipe on an artificial reef. The rough
surfaces help sponges and corals
to become attached.

DID YOU KNOW?

The world's largest
artificial reef was
created when the
aircraft carrier *USS
Oriskany* was sunk
off the coast of
Florida in 2006.

Squirrel fish

Using ocean power

One way to stop global warming is to use renewable sources of energy, such as the sun, wind, and water, instead of coal, oil, and gas. Oceans offer a source of wind, wave, and tidal power.

Wind power at sea

It is often windy at sea, so wind farms (right) can be built in shallow water near coasts. Electricity created by wind turbines is carried to the shore by underwater cables.

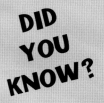

DID YOU KNOW?

There are 20 turbines on the Middelgrunden wind farm off Copenhagen Harbor in Denmark. They supply 5 percent of the electricity needed by the city.

Wave power

Waves smash against the coasts with great energy. In this wave power station (above), the water is forced down a narrow channel and spins a turbine, which generates electricity.

Effects on birdlife

Planners have to be careful when choosing where to build an offshore wind farm. It must not be on bird migration routes or too close to seabird colonies.

Effects on sea life

It is important to make sure that wave power stations and wind farms do not harm the habitats of marine animals, such as porpoises (above), or damage the seabed.

This wind farm is off the coast of Denmark.

Protecting oceans

There are many ways to protect oceans. Beaches where turtles and other marine animals breed can be safeguarded. International laws can protect whales and dolphins, and coral reefs can be made into nature reserves.

Studying the oceans

There is a lot to learn about the world's oceans. People have only just started to explore the deepest parts. By studying the oceans, scientists will be able to find ways of protecting them for the future.

Ocean parks

Important areas of the oceans, such as coral reefs and fish breeding grounds, can be made into marine nature reserves. Here, all animals and plants are protected and fishing is banned.

A helping hand

Many baby turtles die on beaches before they even reach the sea. One way to make sure more survive is to collect turtle eggs (right) and keep them safe until the tiny turtles hatch. The baby turtles are then taken straight out to the sea.

Ecotourism

People love to watch whales and dolphins, and to dive on coral reefs. By protecting ocean life, local people may be able to earn money from tourism instead of from industries that harm the environment.

DID YOU KNOW?

The world's largest marine reserve is being planned. It will stretch for about 1,400 miles (2,200 km) along a chain of islands, north of the Hawaiian Islands, in the Pacific.

Some useful words

Abyss
The bottom of the deep ocean, usually deeper than 5,750 feet (1,755 m).

Bill
The beak of a bird.

Bird
A warm-blooded animal with a body covered in feathers, and with wings instead of arms. Female birds lay eggs.

Bivalve
A mollusk that has two shells, which are hinged together.

Camouflage
A special coloring and body shape that blends with the surroundings, so that an animal is not easily seen by either predators or prey.

Carcass
The dead body of an animal.

Carnivore
An animal that eats other animals.

Colony
A group of animals living together.

Creek
A small stream.

Crest
The very top of a wave.

Cylindrical
Tube-shaped.

Debris
The remains of something that has been broken into pieces.

Environment
The wider surroundings in which an animal or plant lives.

Equator
An imaginary line that runs around the Earth's surface, halfway between the two poles.

Estuary
A place where a river meets the sea and where salt water from the sea mixes with the fresh water of the river.

Fin
A part of the body of a fish that is used for swimming.

Frond
The leaflike part of a seaweed.

Gill
The parts of the body used by fish and some other animals that allow them to them breathe underwater.

Graze
Eat grasses and other plants.

Habitat
The name given to the place where an animal or plant lives.

Horizon
The line in the distance that appears to separate the sky from the sea or land.

Hydrothermal vents
Places on the deep seabed where super-hot water gushes out of gaps in the rocks.

Iceberg
A floating mass of ice.

Invertebrate
An animal that does not have a backbone.

Lagoon
An area of salty water cut off from the sea by a bank of shingle, sand, or coral.

Larva
The growing stage of an animal, such as a young fish or squid.

Mammal
A warm-blooded animal. Female mammals give birth to live young and feed them with their own milk.

Mangrove
Trees that grow along muddy coastlines in warm parts of the world.

Marine
To do with the sea.

Microscopic
Too small to be seen with the naked eye.

Migration
A regular journey made by an animal, sometimes over very long distances.

Mollusk
An animal with a soft body, usually protected by an outer shell.

Molt
Lose hair, feathers, or a shell in order to grow new ones.

Nursery
A place where young animals live while they are growing up.

Nutrient
A substance that is needed for healthy growth and living.

Organism
A living thing, such as an animal, plant, fungus, or bacterium.

Plankton
The tiny plants and animals that are found floating close to the surface of ponds, lakes, and seas.

Polar
To do with the areas around the North and South Poles.

Population
The number of individuals living in a particular area.

Predator
An animal that hunts and feeds on other animals.

Prey
An animal that is hunted by other animals.

Reptile
A cold-blooded animal with a backbone and scaly skin that lays its eggs on dry ground.

Reproduce
Breed, or have babies.

Scale
A small, platelike structure that is found on the skin of reptiles and fish.

Scavenger
An animal that feeds on the bodies of dead animals.

Sedentary
Staying in one place or area without moving.

Sewage
The watery waste from toilets.

Sextant
A mechanical instrument, mainly used in the past by sailors. It is used to measure the postion of the Sun, the Moon, or the stars. From this, sailors can work out where they are.

Shingle
Gravel and small stones.

Shingle bank
A pile of shingle washed onto a beach.

Shoal
A group of fish that swim together.

Solitary
A plant or animal that lives alone.

Sonar
A way of finding the position of objects or prey by using sound waves that travel through the water.

Spawn
Release a lot of small eggs, such as fish or frogs do.

Structure
The way something is built or put together.

Stun
Shock or knock out.

Tentacle
A long, feelerlike structure found on certain animals, such as anemones, jellyfish, and squid.

Titanium
A silvery gray metal.

Tornado
A powerful spinning column of air that forms from a storm cloud and is very destructive.

Vertebrate
An animal that has a backbone.

Wading
Walking in shallow water.

WEB SITES

Parragon does not accept responsibility for the content of any Web sites mentioned in this publication. If you have any questions about their content, please refer to the organization that produced the Web site. If you are under 18, the Web sites mentioned should only be used with the involvement of a parent or guardian.

http://www.noaa.gov/
Web site of the U.S. National Oceanic and Atmospheric Administration.

http://www.mbayaq.org/
The Monterey Bay Aquarium in California.

http://www.whoi.edu
The Woods Hole Oceanographic Institution.

http://www.panda.org/about_wwf/
what_we_do/marine/index.cfm
The WWF (formerly the World Wildlife Fund).

http://www.wdcs.org/
The Whale and Dolphin Conservation Society.

http://www.coralreefalliance.org/
The Coral Reef Alliance.

Index

A

albatrosses 23, 184–85
algae 40, 89, 100, 110, 169
alligators 55
amphipods 33, 64, 117, 146, 147
anglerfish 147
Antarctica 165–67, 176, 188–89
aquatic animals 24–25
arches 37
Arctic 165–89, 208
Arctic foxes 172
Arctic Ocean 10, 11, 82, 165, 169, 174–75
Arctic terns 186, 187
arrow crabs 108
astrolabe 13
Atlantic Ocean 10, 13, 19, 33, 123, 161, 162
atolls 92, 93
aurorae 167

B

bacteria 147, 202
baleen whales 66, 80–81
barnacles 38
barracudas 102, 103
beaches 28, 35, 36, 44–49
    nests 44, 58–59, 214
    pollution 199, 200, 203, 204
bears 49, 172, 182–83, 208

beluga whales 82, 180
bioluminescence 33, 63, 125, 137, 142, 147, 149
birds 19, 68, 144, 201, 213
    bills 51, 52
    coastal 42, 43, 61, 78–79
    polar 184–87
    waders 17, 51, 52
birds of prey 57
bivalves 110
black smokers 162
bleaching 210
blennies 39
blizzards 166
blobfish 158
blowholes 80
blubber 173, 178
blue whales 66, 80, 81
boats, see ships and boats
body armor 106, 107
bow waves 15
breakers 14
breathing 24, 25, 30, 56, 80, 115, 179
breeding 77, 84–85, 108, 133, 135, 173
brittle stars 141, 155
butterfly fish 101

C

camouflage 82, 98, 106, 107, 125, 182
carbon dioxide 209
cardinal fish 108, 109
Caribbean Sea 10, 19, 88
caves 37
chronometer 12
clams 74, 110, 111

cliffs 35, 36, 42–43, 78
    deep-ocean 160–61
clown fish 98
coastal waters 61–85
coasts 35–59, 199
cockles 47, 53
coconuts 44
cod 123, 168, 175
comb jellies 33, 116
conservation 196–97, 211, 214–15
continental shelf 28
Cook, Captain James 13
copepods 64, 117, 136, 168, 169
coral 90, 94–97, 99, 100–101
coral reefs 11, 31, 87–111, 214
    artificial 211
    deep-sea 161
    dying 208, 210–11
    exposed 89
    reef animals 100–111
    types 92–93
cormorants 79
cowfish 107
crabs 24, 29, 38, 48, 57, 59, 98, 108, 151, 160
currents 18–19, 134

D

dark zone 140, 141
Dead Sea 23
deep ocean 32–33, 141, 146–49, 158–63
defenses 106–7
deltas 50

diatoms 62
dinoflagellates 63
divers 30–31, 73, 140, 205, 211
dolphins 27, 83, 120, 132–33, 141, 198, 204, 205

E

earthquakes 14
echolocation 132
eels 91, 99, 135, 146–47
Egyptians, ancient 12
electricity 212
endangered species 123, 174, 193, 196–97
energy 209, 212–13
equator 18, 20, 56
estuaries 50–51, 53
explorers 12–13, 32, 214

F

fan worms 153
fangtooth 143
farming fish 194–95
Faroe Islands 207
feather stars 90
fiddler crabs 57
filter feeders 66–67, 80–81
fish 19, 24, 27
    baby fish 64, 135
    coastal 54, 74, 75, 202
    conservation 196–97
    deep-sea 158–59
    as food 191, 193, 197
    giant 128–29
    hunters 126–27
    poisonous 46
    reef 98–103, 106–9

tidal pools 39
    shoals 120–21, 123, 196
fish farms 194–95
fishing 122–24, 189, 192–93, 196–97
fishing nets 122, 123, 192, 193, 196, 197
    trapped animals 204, 205
flatfish 53
flippers 25
flying fish 114
food chains 26–27, 121, 124
frog fish 107

G

Galápagos Islands 39
gannets 43, 78–79
garbage 191, 202–4, 211
garibaldi fish 75
geese 186, 187
ghost crabs 48
giant clams 110, 111
giant squid 144, 148–49
gills 24, 56, 66
global warming 191, 208–9, 210
gobies 106
gravity 16
Great Barrier Reef 89
greenhouse gases 209
groins 36
Gulf Stream 19
gulls 19, 79

H

hagfish 155
hammerhead shark 29, 84
Harrison, John 12
hatchetfish 142

hawksbill turtles 100, 131
hermit crabs 98
herring 196
high tide 16, 36, 47, 48
horseshoe crabs 59
hot-water vents 22, 162–63
humpback whales 66, 81, 85, 115, 180
hurricanes 20, 57

I

ice 165–69, 172–73, 208
ice fish 174
icebergs 10, 170–71
igloos 188
iguanas, marine 39
Indian Ocean 10, 11, 21, 88, 92
Inuit people 188
islands 11, 92

J K

jellyfish 25, 65, 118–19, 175
kelp forests 72–75
killer whales, see orcas
krill 68–69, 79, 81, 168

L

lagoons 92
lantern fish 137
larvae 64, 117, 163
limpets 40, 41, 74
lion fish 103
lion's mane jellyfish 119
lizard fish 102
lobsters 77
low tide 16, 17, 47, 89
lugworms 52

M

manatees 76, 198
mangrove swamps 35, 56–57, 195
manta rays 67, 85, 128
maps 12, 33
Mariana Trench 29, 33
marlin 126
marshes 54–55
Mediterranean Sea 10, 12
medusa 146
megamouth sharks 145
mermaid's purses 105
Mid-Atlantic Ridge 33
migration 85, 131, 135, 136
mollusks 110–11
monsoon 21
Moon 16
moray eels 91, 99
mountains 33
mudflats 35, 50–53
mudskippers 56
mussels 40, 163

N

narwhals 82, 180
nature reserves 214, 215
nautilus 142
navigation 12, 13
nests 43, 58, 59, 75
Nile Delta 50
nocturnal animals 108–109
nudibranches 111
nurseries 84–85, 135

O

ocean layers 140
octopus 103
oil spills 200–1
open ocean 113–37
orcas 82, 83, 181
ospreys 57
overfishing 123, 174, 191, 192–93, 196, 210
oystercatchers 17, 52

P

Pacific Ocean 10, 11, 13, 29, 39, 88, 92, 184
parasites 81, 99, 152
parrot fish 100
pelicans 26, 27, 78
penguins 68, 144, 166, 176–77
people 188–89, 191
phytoplankton 26, 62–63
plankton 19, 26, 61, 62–67, 80–81, 97, 140, 154
plants 42, 54, 55
plastic bags 204, 205
poison 46, 103, 107, 111
polar bears 172, 182–83, 208
polar regions 165–89
pollution 191, 194, 199, 210
   oil spills 200–201
porpoises 83, 213
Portuguese man-of-war 116
power stations 209, 212–13
puffins 42, 43

R

Raleigh, Sir Walter 13
rat-tails 159
rays 67, 74, 85, 128
razor shells 47
reefs, see coral reefs
regeneration 157
remotely operated vehicles (ROVs) 32
renewable energy 212–13
reptiles 39, 55
rivers 50, 88
rocks 36, 37, 38–42, 44

S

sailfish 127
salmon farms 194, 195
salps 65
salt marshes 54–55
salt pans 22
salt water 22–23, 54
sand 36, 37, 44–47, 93, 100
sand dollars 46
sand dunes 45
sandhoppers 49
sardines 121
Sargasso Sea 134–35
scavengers 48–49, 108
scientists 32, 33, 188, 189, 214
sea anemones 41, 98, 160
seabed 28–29, 33, 150–59, 203
seabirds, see birds
sea butterfly 174
sea grass 76–77
sea horses 77, 106
sea ice 168–69

sea levels 208

sea lilies 157

sealions 28

seals 17, 25, 44, 69, 145, 169, 173, 178–79

sea nettles 119

sea otters 51, 74, 75

sea pens 150

sea slugs 151

sea urchins 73, 74, 150

seaweed 38, 39, 48, 70–75, 134, 140

sewage 202, 203

shark fishing 193

sharks 74, 128
  breathing 24
  breeding 84, 105
  deep-water 29, 145, 158, 159
  food chains 26, 27, 61
  hunters 127
  plankton feeders 66, 67
  reef 104–5, 208

shells 45, 53, 98, 110

shingle 36, 54

ships and boats 12, 15, 115, 198, 203

shipwrecks 31, 93, 199, 211

shores 14, 15, 35–59

shrimp 54, 99, 136, 143, 162, 163, 195

siphonophores 116, 117

snails 38, 46, 51, 53, 110, 111

snappers 109

snipe eels 146

sonar 198

Southern Ocean 10, 165, 174, 176, 184

sperm whales 141, 144

spider crabs 29, 151

spits 37

sponges 91, 100, 160, 211

squid 69, 84, 117, 124–25, 148–49

squirrel fish 109

starfish 28, 38, 47, 101, 156–57

stings 46, 96, 97, 98, 117, 118–19, 150

storms 20, 72, 115

strand line 48–49

submarines 198

submersibles 32

Sun 16, 167

sunfish 129

sunlight 114, 136, 140–41

sunstars 156

surface layer 114–17, 136, 140

surfing 15, 83

swamps 54–57

swans 187

swordfish 126

T

tapeworms 152

tidal pools 38, 39, 41

tidal zones 47

tides 16–17, 36, 37, 44, 202

Titanic 171

tourism 215

transport 191, 198–99

trawlers 122–23, 192, 193

tropical storms 20

tropics 20, 44, 56

trout 194

tsunamis 14, 15, 57

tube worms 163

tuna 123, 137

turtles 23, 58, 100, 130–31, 204, 205, 215

twilight zone 140, 142–45

V W Z

volcanoes 22, 92

wading birds 17, 51, 52

wahoos 129

walruses 173, 179

waste 191, 202–4

water pressure 32, 140

water spouts 21

wave power 212–13

waves 14, 36, 44, 48, 115

weather 20–21

weaver fish 46

whales 66, 68, 85, 115, 204, 205
  baleen whales 80–81
  deep-water 141, 144
  feeding 66, 68, 79
  polar 82, 180–81
  stranded 198, 199
  toothed 82–83

whaling 206–7

wind 42, 45, 168
  storms 20–21, 166
  waves and currents 14, 18, 115

wind farms 212–13

wolf fish 161

worms 51, 52, 152–53

zooplankton 26, 61, 64–65

Acknowledgments

Artwork supplied by Peter Bull, The Art Agency.

Photo credits:
b = bottom, t = top, r = right, l = left, c = center

Cover images:
Front: br Herbert Kehrer/zefa/CORBIS, bc Arthur Morris/CORBIS, bl Hal Beral/zefa/CORBIS, c Mark A. Johnson/CORBIS, tr Stephen Frink/GETTY IMAGES, tc Tom Brakefield/CORBIS, tl Arthur Morris/CORBIS.
Back: bl Brandon D. Cole/CORBIS, bc Stuart Westmorland/CORBIS, tl Ralph A. Clevenger/CORBIS, tr Bryan Allen/CORBIS.
Spine: Ralph A. Clevenger/CORBIS.

1 Dreamstime.com/Mikhail Blajenov, 2-3 Stephen Frink/Corbis, 4-5 Stuart Westmorland/Corbis, 6tl Dreamstime.com/Nikolay Alexandrov, 6tr Dreamstime.com, 6c Dreamstime.com, 6bl Dreamstime.com/John Abramo, 6br Dreamstime.com, 7t istockphoto.com/Tore Johannesen, 7b Dreamstime.com/David Lloyd, 8–9 Stuart Westmorland/Corbis, 10tl Dreamstime.com/Jan Will, 11tr Dreamstime.com/Wolfgang Amri, 11b Dreamstime.com/Matthias Weinrich, 12tr Bettmann/CORBIS, 12b Dreamstime.com, 13bl istockphoto.com/ Adam Booth, 12bm National Archive of Canada, 14t Dreamstime.com, 14-15b istockphoto.com, 15t Goebel/zefa/Corbis, 15m Dreamstime.com/Lucila De Avila, 16tl Dreamstime.com, 17t Dreamstime.com/Caroline Henri, 17b Dreamstime.com/Mark Ross, 18b Dreamstime.com/Peter Elvidge, 19b Dreamstime.com, 20-21 Dreamstime.com/Matthew Scholey, 20cl NASA, 21tr Harish Tyagi/epa/Corbis, 21b NOAA, 22l Dreamstime.com/Simon Gurney, 22b Digital Vision, 23tl Digital Vision, 23b Digital Vision, 24-25t Dreamstime.com/Ian Scott, 24b Dreamstime.com/Stacy Barnett, 25tr Dreamstime.com/Cathy Figuli, 25b Dreamstime.com/Andrea Leone, 26bl Dreamstime.com, 27t Chris & Monique Fallows/OceanwideImages.com, 27bl Dreamstime.com/Miguel Angelo Silva, 27br Dreamstime.com/Laurin Rinder, 28cl Dreamstime.com/Jan Martin Will, 28br Dreamstime.com/Igor Groshev, 29t Dreamstime.com/John Stublar, 30tr Dreamstime.com/Linda Bucklin, 30b Dreamstime.com/Nick Poling, 31tl Dreamstime.com/Simon Gurney, 31b Stephen Frink/Corbis, 32tl Ralph White/CORBIS, 32b Ralph White/CORBIS, 33m all NOAA, 34-35 Martin Harvey/Corbis, 36l Dreamstime.com/Anna Karwowska, 36br Dreamstime.com/Peter Clark, 37t Dreamstime.com/Joe Gough, 37b NASA, 38t istockphoto.com, 38b Dreamstime.com/Publicimage, 39tl Dreamstime.com, 39r Dreamstime.com/Michael Johnson Jr, 40t Dreamstime.com/Stuart Key, 40b Dreamstime.com/Jay Prescott, 41t Bob Rowan; Progressive Image/CORBIS, 41b Dreamstime.com, 42-43 Dreamstime.com/Imagecd.co.uk, 42b Dreamstime.com/Jesse, 43t Dreamstime.com/Darryl Sleath, 43b Dreamstime.com/Gail Johnson, 44-45 Dreamstime.com/Mikhail Matsonashvili, 44br Dreamstime.com/Dmitry Pichugin, 45t Dreamstime.com/Elena Elisseeva, 45b Dreamstime.com/Nikolay Dimitrov, 46tl Dreamstime.com, 46br Lawson Wood/CORBIS, 47b Stuart Westmorland/CORBIS, 48-49 Dreamstime.com/Robert Adrian Hillman, 48b Dreamstime.com/Nico Smit, 49t Robin Williams; Ecoscene/CORBIS, 49b Dreamstime.com/Randy Harris, 50l NASA, 50b Yann Arthus-Bertrand/CORBIS, 51t Dreamstime.com/Sandy Matzen, 51b Dreamstime.com, 52b Dreamstime.com/Stefan Ekernas, 53t Dreamstime.com/Dragoneye, 53b Dreamstime.com/Heather Jones, 54t Dreamstime.com/Dmitrijs Mihejevs, 54b Dreamstime.com/Emilia Kun, 55t Marco Schmidt, 55b Dreamstime.com/Stefan Ekernas, 56-57 Dreamstime.com/Daniel Gustavsson, 56b Dreamstime.com/Anthony J. Hall, 57t Dreamstime.com/Jeff Gynane, 57b Dreamstime.co/Anthony Hall, 58t Dreamstime.com, 58b Paulo Whitaker/Reuters/Corbis, 59t Dreamstime.com/Jessica Fitzel, 59cl Roger Garwood and Trish Ainslie/CORBIS, 59br Dreamstime.com/Steffen Foerster, 60-61 Stephen Frink/Corbis, 62cl Visuals Unlimited/ Corbis, 63tl Douglas P. Wilson; Frank Lane Picture Agency/CORBIS, 63r NASA, 64 cl Uwe Kils, 65tr istockphoto.com, 65b NOAA, 66tl Brandon D. Cole/CORBIS, 66bc NOAA, 66-67b istockphoto.com/ Klaas Lingbeek-van Kranen, 67t Dreamstime.com/Harald Bolten, 68b Dreamstime.com/Bernard Beton, 69t Dreamstime.com/Jan Will, 69b NOAA, 70tl Dreamstime.com, 70-71 Dreamstime.com, 71tl Dreamstime.com, 71tc Dreamstime.com, 71tr Dreamstime.com/Marcel Nijhuis, 71br Dreamstime.com/Radu Razvan, 72l and bc Dreamstime.com/Jeff Waibel, 73l Jeffrey L. Rotman/CORBIS, 73tr Dreamstime.com/Chris Ryan, 73br Dreamstime.com, 74c istockphoto.com, 74bl Dreamstime.com, 75tll istockphoto.com, 75 Dreamstime.com, 76-77 Stuart Westmorland/Corbis, 76bl Dreamstime.com/Dejan Sarman, 77bl Jeffrey L. Rotman/CORBIS, 77r Dreamstime.com/Steffen Foerster, 78bl Dreamstime.com/Fotograf77, 78-79t Dreamstime.com/David Lloyd, 79cl Dreamstime.com/Anita Huszti, 79br istockphoto.com, 80tl DK Limited/CORBIS, 80cr Dreamstime.com/Ken Moore, 80b Dreamstime.com/Eric Isselée, 81b Dreamstime.com/Brett Atkins, 82cl istockphoto.com/Sandra Minarik, 82b istockphoto.com, 83t istockphoto.com/Adam White, 83bl Theo Allofs/Corbis, 84tr CORBIS SYGMA, 84bl istockphoto.com, 84br Wolfgang Kaehler/CORBIS, 85t istockphoto.com, 86-87 Stuart Westmorland/Corbis, 88-89t istockphoto.com, 89bl Dreamstime.com/Chinieh, 89cr Dreamstime.com/Duard Van Der Westhuizen, 90tl NOAA, 90b Dreamstime.com/ Asther Lau Choon Siew, 91t Dreamstime.com/John Abramo, 91b Dreamstime.com/John Anderson, 92cr NASA, 93tl Dreamstime.com, 93r Dreamstime.com/Holger Wulschlaeger, 94tr istockphoto.com, 94b Dreamstime.com/Asther Lau choon siew, 95t Dreamstime.com/Asther Lau choon siew, 95b Jeffrey L. Rotman/CORBIS, 96t Dreamstime.com, 96b istockphoto.com/Adam Schneider, 97 istockphoto.com, 97br Dreamstime.com/Dirk-jan Mattaar, 98t Dreamstime.com/Andrea Leone, 98bl Brandon D. Cole/CORBIS, 99tr Stephen Frink/CORBIS, 99b istockphoto.com, 100tr and 101tr Dreamstime.com/Mikhail Blajenov, 100bl istockphoto.com/Dan Schmitt, 101tl Dreamstime.com/Asther Lau choon siew, 101br David Burdick, 102t Dreamstime.com, Beverly Speed, 102tl Dreamstime.com/Asther Lau choon siew, 102bl Dreamstime.com/Cornelis Opstal, 103t Dreamstime.com/Wei Send Chen, 103br istockphoto.com/ Dan Schmitt, 104cr Dreamstime.com/Olga Khoroshunova, 104b NOAA, 105t istockphoto.com/Chris Dascher, 105b Douglas P. Wilson; Frank Lane Picture Agency/CORBIS, 106tr istockphoto.com/RbbrDckyBK, 106b Dreamstime.com, 107t Dreamstime.com/Olga Khoroshunova, 107cr Dreamstime.com/Franky, 108tr Dreamstime.com/memm74, 108b Dreamstime.com/Dennis Sabo, 109tr istockphoto.com, 109bl NOAA, 110tl istockphoto.com, 110b Dreamstime.com/Asther Lau choon siew, 111tl Dreamstime.com/Kwerry, 111r Dreamstime.com/Cornelis Opstal, 112-113 W. Perry Conway/CORBIS, 114t Dreamstime.com/Sergey Galushko , 114cl Tony Arruza/CORBIS, 114-115b Dreamsitme.com/Darren Baker, 115tr NOAA, 116l NOAA, 116b Dreamstime.com/John Wollwerth, 117tr NOAA, 117bl NOAA, 118t Dreamstime.com/Cathy Figuli, 118b Dreamstime.com/Nick Edens, 119tr Kip Evans, 119b Dreamstime.com/Alexei Novikov, 120-121 Dreamstime.com, 120bl Dreamstime.com/Brett Atkins, 121tr Dreamstime.com/Tommy Schultz, 121br istockphoto.com/David Safanda, 122tr Digital Vision, 122b Dreamstime.com/Roman Kazmin, 123t NOAA, 123cl Dreamstime.com/Steinar Figved, 124-125t Dreamstime.com/Inga Ivanova, 124bl Dreamstime.com/Asther Lau Choon Siew, 125cl Dreamstime.com/Asther Lau Choon Siew, 125bl istockphoto.com/Paul Topp, 126-127 Bob Gomel/CORBIS, 126cl istockphoto.com/Luis Carlos Torres, 127t NOAA, 127b Dreamstime.com/Roman Dekan, 128-129 Amos Nachoum/CORBIS, 128bl Dreasmtime.com/Martin Strmko, 129tr istockphoto.com/Chuck Babbitt, 129br NOAA, 130t Digital Vision, 130b Dreamstime.com/Tommy Schultz, 131tr Digital Vision, 131b Dreamstime.com/David Lloyd, 132t istockphoto.com/Kristian Sekulic, 132-133 Stuart Westmorland/CORBIS, 133t istockphoto.com, 134-135t NOAA, 135t Dreamstime.com/ Mikhail Blajenov, 135cr Uwe Kils, 135bl Uwe Kils, 136cr NOAA, 137 Peter Herring/imagequestmarine.com, 137bl NOAA, 138-139 Ralph White/CORBIS, 140 Denis Scott/Corbis, 141t Dreamstime.com/Lenets Sergey, 141b NOAA, 142tr NOAA, 142b istockphoto.com/Charles Babbitt, 143tr NOAA, 144tr Dreamstime.com/Stephan Zabel, 144-145 Rick Price/CORBIS, 145br NOAA, 146tl Peter Parks/imagequestmarine.com, 146b NOAA, 148cl NOAA, 148tr NOAA, 148-149 Visuals Unlimited/Corbis, 149br New Zealand Ministry of Fisheries/Handout/epa/Corbis, 150tr USGS, 150b NOAA, 151t Dreamstime.com/Asther Lau Choon Siew, 152tr Stephen Frink/CORBIS, 153t NOAA, 154t NOAA, 154b NOAA, 155t Brandon D. Cole/CORBIS, 156tl NOAA, 156cr NOAA, 156br NOAA, 157tl Dreamstime.com/Jill Maroo, 157tr Dreamstime.com/Asther Lau Choon Siew, 157bl NOAA, 158bl NOAA, 159t Stuart Westmorland/CORBIS, 159cl NOAA, 160tl NOAA, 160bl NOAA, 161t NOAA, 161b NOAA, 162cl NOAA, 162b NOAA, 163tr NOAA, 163tc NOAA, 163cr NOAA, 164-165 Jenny E. Ross/Corbis, 166tl NASA, 166-167b Tim Davis/CORBIS, 167tr istockphoto.com, 167cl Dreamstime.com/Luke Pederson, 168t Dreamstime.com, 168bl Rick Price/CORBIS, 169tl NOAA, 169b Dreamstime.com/Natalia Bratslavsky, 170cr NASA 170-171 Wolfgang Kaehler/CORBIS, 171br NOAA, 172tl istockphoto.com/John Pitcher, 172b istockphoto.com/Dmitry Deshevykh, 173 NOAA, 173cl Dreamstime.com/Kwerry, 174cl NOAA, 174-175 Rick Price/CORBIS, 175 NOAA, 175 Dreamstime.com, 176tl Dreamstime.com/Olga Solovei, 176-177 Dreamstime.com/Bernard Breton, 177tr istockphoto.com/Alexander Hafemann, 177br Dreamtime.com/Vladimir Seliverstov, 178-179t Dreamstime.com/Jeff Goldman, 178bl istockphoto.com, 179tr Dreamstime.com/Vladimir Seliverstov, 179bl Dreamstime.com/ Nikolay Alexandrov, 180tl istockphoto.com/Klaas Lingbeek van Kranen, 180b NOAA, 181t Dreamstime.com, 181bl NOAA, 182tr Dreamstime.com/Anthony Hathaway, 182b istockphoto.com/Stefan Klein, 183t Dreamstime.com/Gail Johnson, 183b istockphoto.com/John Pitcher, 184l Dreamstime.com/Vladimir Seliverstov, 184br Dreamstime.com/Oystein Sando, 185tl Paul Souders/Corbis, 185b istockphoto.com/Richard Waghorn, 186tl Dreamstime.com/Roy Longmuir, 186bl istockphoto.com/Roger Whiteway, 186-187 istockphoto.com/Mikhail Soldatenkov, 187tr Dreamstime.com/Aaron Whitney, 188tr Dreamstime.com/Andrew Buckin, 188-189b Roger Tidman/CORBIS, 189b NOAA, 190-191 Bettmann/CORBIS, 192-193 Natalie Fobes/CORBIS, 192b Dreamstime.com/Dragan Cvetanovic, 193tr istockphoto.com/John Peacock, 193cr istockphoto.com/Lim Weng Chai, 194cl Dreamstime.com/David Hyde, 194cr Dreamstime.com/Irochka, 194br istockphoto.com/Arne Thaysen, 194-195 Kevin Fleming/CORBIS, 195tr Chaiwat Subprasom/Reuters/Corbis, 195c istockphoto.com/Amanda Rohde, 196cl NOAA, 196-197 istockphoto.com/ Jan Kranendonk, 197tr Dreamstime.com/Kheng Guan Toh, 197br istockphoto.com/Willy Philippo, 198bl Dreamstime.com/Daniel Gale, 198-199 Stuart Westmorland/CORBIS, 199cr and br Dreamstime.com/Joe Gough, 200tr NOAA, 200b Digital Vision, 201tr Chinch Gryniewicz; Ecoscene/CORBIS, 201l Digital Vision, 202-203t Dreamstime.com/Galina Barskaya, 202bl Digital Vision, 203cl Alan Schein Photography/CORBIS, 203cr istockphoto.com/Jonathan White, 204tl Jonathan Blair/CORBIS, 204br Stuart Westmorland/CORBIS, 205t Digital Vision, 205b NOAA, 206cr NOAA, 206br NOAA, 207tr Hulton-Deutsch Collection/CORBIS, 206-207b Jonathan Blair/CORBIS, 208t istockphoto.com/Harald Bolten, 208l Dreamstime.com/Vladimir Seliverstov, 209tr Dreamstime.com/ Tom Davison, 209br istockphoto.com, 210b Dreamstime.com/Asther Lau Choon Siew, 211tl Dreametime.com/Miguel Angelo Silva, 211tr NOAA, 211br NOAA, 212br courtesy of Wavegen, 212-213b istockphoto.com/Tore Johannesen, 213tl Dreamstime.com/Uwe Ohse, 213tr Dreamstime.com/Fairn Whatley, 214tr Dreamstime.com/Alexander Putyata, 214b Dreametime.com, 215ct NOAA, 215tr Dreamstime.com/Paul Cowan, 215cl istockphoto.com/Jurga Rubinovaite.